C000218002

Ruth Pitter was born at Ilford in 1897.
both teachers in the East End, and intr
poetry and to an enjoyment of the c
London. Her first poems appeared in p
when she was still at Coborn School f
helped to publish her *First Poems* in 1920, and subsequent volumes
established her reputation on both sides of the Atlantic as one of the
most distinctive voices in 20th-century poetry: her work was praised
by Yeats and C.S. Lewis, and she was described by Lord David
Cecil as 'the most moving of living English poets, and one of the
most original'. A younger generation of writers, among them
Thom Gunn and John Wain, was equally enthusiastic.

This new volume gathers together the finest of Ruth Pitter's poems,
which in Kathleen Raine's judgement 'will survive as long as the
English language, with whose expressiveness in image and idea she
has kept faith, remains'. In the introduction Elizabeth Jennings
– herself among the most distinguished of contemporary poets –
pays tribute to Pitter's 'acute sensibility and deep integrity' and refers
to her precision in observing Nature, her skill with verse forms
and the frequency with which she achieves a 'beautifully
communicated vision'.

Ruth Pitter received the Hawthornden Prize in 1937, the Heinemann
Award for Literature in 1954 and was the first woman recipient of
the Queen's Gold Medal for Poetry in 1955. She was made a
Companion of Literature in 1974 and a C.B.E. in 1979. For many
years she earned her living as a painter of furniture and of ornamental
trays; after retiring to Long Crendon, Buckinghamshire, she took
up gardening and became known to a wide audience through the
TV *Brains Trust*. She died on 29 February 1992.

Ruth Pitter

COLLECTED POEMS

Introduced
by
Elizabeth Jennings

London
ENITHARMON PRESS
1996

Published in 1996
by the Enitharmon Press
36 St George's Avenue
London N7 0HD

This edition is a revised
version of Ruth Pitter's *Collected Poems (1990)*

ISBN 1 870612 14 0

Set in 10pt Bembo by Bryan Williamson
and printed in an edition of 2000 copies
by the Cromwell Press, Wiltshire

ACKNOWLEDGEMENTS

In preparing this volume the editor wishes to
acknowledge the generous assistance given by
David Austen, Alan Clodd, Professor Peter Dickinson,
Muriel Dickinson, Robert Gardner, Barry Humphries,
Elizabeth Jennings, Marco Livingstone,
Jean R. Milant and Mary Thomas.

BIBLIOGRAPHY

First Poems (London, Cecil Palmer, 1920)

First and Second Poems
(London, Sheed & Ward, 1927; New York, Doubleday Doran, 1930)

Persephone in Hades (Privately printed, 1931)

A Mad Lady's Garland
(London, Cresset Press, 1934; New York, Macmillan, 1935)

A Trophy of Arms: Poems 1926-1935
(London, Cresset Press, 1936; New York, Macmillan, 1936)

The Spirit Watches
(London, Cresset Press, 1939; New York, Macmillan, 1940)

The Rude Potato (London, Cresset Press, 1941)

Poem (Southampton, Shirley Press, 1943)

The Bridge: Poems 1939-1944
(London, Cresset Press, 1945; New York, Macmillan, 1946)

Pitter on Cats (London, Cresset Press, 1947)

Urania (Selection from *A Trophy of Arms, The Spirit Watches* and *The Bridge*,
with title page by Joan Hassall; London, Cresset Press, 1950)

The Ermine: Poems 1942-1952 (London, Cresset Press, 1953)

Still by Choice (London, Cresset Press, 1966)

Poems 1926-1966
(London, Barrie & Rockcliff/The Cresset Press, 1968;
published in New York by Macmillan as *Collected Poems* in 1969)

End of Drought (London, Barrie & Jenkins, 1975)

A Heaven to Find (London, Enitharmon Press, 1987)

Collected Poems (1990) (Petersfield, Enitharmon Press, 1990)

Collected Poems (London, Enitharmon Press, 1996)

FESTSCHRIFT

Ruth Pitter: Homage to a Poet (London, Rapp & Whiting, 1969; edited by
Arthur Russell with an introduction by Lord David Cecil and essays by
Edmund Blunden, Andrew Young, John Arlott, John Betjeman, Richard
Church, Robert Conquest, Roy Fuller, Joyce Grenfell, Mary Grieve, Thom
Gunn, L.P. Hartley, Elizabeth Jennings, P.J. Kavanagh, James Kirkup,
Carolyn Kizer, Stanley Kunitz, Naomi Lewis, Rupert Bruce Lockhart,
Edward Lucie-Smith, Dame Ngaio Marsh, Derek Parker, Kathleen Raine,
Robin Skelton, Robert Speaight, Hallam Tennyson, John Wain and John
Hall Wheelock).

CONTENTS

9

10

12

13

A Heaven to Find is a selection of unpublished poems and fragments of poems written between 1908 and 1976.

INTRODUCTION

While re-reading the work of Ruth Pitter, written over more than half a century, I was immediately struck by her acute sensibility and deep integrity. It does therefore seem important to say here something about the place of morality in poetry; by morality I mean a profoundly humane attitude towards the world in general and an honesty so large that it becomes a celebration of truth itself. I also mean a humility which, like Eliot's simplicity, costs "not less than everything". A poet must, too, possess a sense of vocation which entails a willingness to face arid times when no poems are written. These have to be endured if one is ever to know those rare moments when a poem really seems to succeed. Lastly, a fastidious commitment is vital to artists in any medium.

The poems of Ruth Pitter are informed with a sweetness which is also bracing, and a generosity which is blind to nothing, neither the sufferings in this world nor the quirky behaviour of human beings; indeed, she rather enjoys the latter. Her introduction to her *Poems 1926-66* is a marvellously illuminating essay which tells us most lucidly her own views on the art of writing poems. She was brought up to love the art and started writing herself when she was "about five" but she says that she "produced little that I now think worth keeping until the age of thirty." Of this long early growth within her she has something to say that probably only a visionary poet, which she often is, though not always, could declare with conviction. She mourns the loss "of the glory of this long immaturity. It produced artless art, but it was a wonderful mode of life."

Ruth Pitter goes on to tell us of her lofty view of poetry. For her, it has been a life-long passion and she was ready to sacrifice money, security, luxury and all "consolations" in fact, to attain "the ineffable communion with the earth itself." She has, however, a highly-developed sense of humour and admits ruefully that, though she has always tried to be "kind" to others, she has often felt her gift "privately boiling with these disgraceful rancours which are the exhaust-fumes of ruling passions." Since childhood, writing poems has meant for Ruth Pitter an attempt to "express something of the secret meanings which haunt life and language." She goes on to speak of "the silent music, the dance in stillness" which resides in all things, whether "the smile on the face of the tiger or the Bernini seraph."

She believes that this silence (she would surely agree that there is indeed a music of the spheres) is also unconsciously present in all of us; it is the poet's task to capture it and hold it down, to find words for what seems inexpressible, to pack imagery with the slightest nuance which suggests order in the many contradictions of creation. Making a poem is a mysterious act; poets and critics have always tried to define it but no-one has ever been able to catch it in one simple phrase. Ruth Pitter says that "It begins in that secret movement of the poet's being in response to the secret dynamism of life." Probably no poem quite lives up to that sudden excitement, that fruitful moment when one does genuinely feel almost taken over by what one is writing and when the pen cannot move fast enough.

But Ruth Pitter is well aware of the poet's wrestle with craftsmanship, the battle with a medium which uses "the legal tender and common currency of language." The poem, she declares "may emerge clear of hocus-pocus." There is nothing pompous about this; the poem is "a structure" but the finer summits of great verse are "shiftingly veiled... yet they have *seen something*." A poem may be, she continues "a squib, a satire... a noble sermon or a Chinese puzzle." This poet is not scornful about the lower reaches, as it were, of verse; she knows very well that even the greatest poets only reach the heights occasionally. The poet must, however, always be ready for visitations, not seek them out but keep his craftsmanship untarnished, his imagination uncluttered by wasteful thoughts. Those rare moments which seem like revelations are, Ruth Pitter says, the poet's "chief aim and justification."

In short, poems spring from "beatitude and anguish" but Ruth Pitter finds that the comic spirit is also of great importance. As we know, lack of humour can betray a poet into writing verse which is unwittingly funny. Wordsworth is the obvious example of this. A sense of the comic can be a harmonising factor; it eschews egotism and insists on objectivity.

From her earliest published work, Ruth Pitter has shown herself to be a fine botanist and ornithologist and her Nature poetry has become, with each new book, more detailed, precise and vivid.

In the early work we never find faulty craftsmanship but there is at times a tendency to generalise and a use of archaisms which disappears fairly rapidly with each new book. Ruth Pitter's skill with a variety of verse forms, rhymed and unrhymed, is always evident. As she becomes more adept at making her subjects and themes inseparable from form and music, so her observations of Nature appear more exact and more simple; the very titles of her poems show this: 'The Cygnet', 'The Crow', 'Wild Honey', 'The Estuary', 'The Ermine' are but a few examples. Perhaps paradoxically, the closer she keeps to the life of natural creatures, the more frequent does the visionary element in her work appear. This can only be shown by quotation. 'The Bird in the Tree', with its wonderful simplicity of language and rhythm in five short-lined quatrains, reaches an inevitable conclusion which almost takes one's breath away:

> O give me before I die
>   The grace to see
> With eternal, ultimate eye,
>   The Bird and the Tree.
>
> The song in the living green,
>   The Tree and the Bird –
> O have they ever been seen,
>   Ever been heard?

There are a great number of poems which achieve this beautifully communicated vision. Here that "silent music" is caught and conveyed to us. A later poem called 'Morning Glory' examines various ways of looking at a flower and then finally breaks into the thoroughly earned flight of "A prescient tingling, a prophecy of sound." This is the mystery or magic of poetry which can never be sought and also never be faked.

Ruth Pitter's style may often appear simple but this is a hard-won simplicity of tone, of form, a simplicity which leads to the profound. The depths and the heights of the human spirit are never expressed in complexity. She is aware of many great truths. Her mind works upon the contradictions in Christianity and in the forces of Nature. Her own intellect and spirit must have known many battles to enable her to arrive at felicities such as these:

> The implacable and humble need,

17

The spell, the prayer, the proud pavane,
Conceived before those hills began.
                              ('The Small Plant')

What does each Adoration care
For sorrow measured off by sound?
                              ('Old Clockwork Time')

I that am born must come to be
Right as are the shells from sea;
And the bitter snow is calling me
To come through sorrow to charity.
                              ('The Chimneypiece')

Ruth Pitter has also written love poems and poems about "the illumination of the soul", such as 'Passion and Peace' which opens with the line "Poetry, like all passion, seeks for peace" and ends

O let the fervour of the princely sun,
Which makes the desert solitary, sleep
Here in the water his dominions weep,
Binding all peace and passion into one.

She can also draw from a flower an almost rapturous statement as in these lines which end 'Flowers in the Factory':

How the Jonquil's tender face,
Like a spirit sent to save,
Like a love discovered in a dreadful place
Lights a candle in the cruel grave.

Over years of dedicated craftsmanship Ruth Pitter has increased her formal dexterity and varied her ways of turning that "silent music", which she has spoken of so eloquently, into lucid and memorable sound informed by original thought. She is a very difficult poet to paraphrase because her meaning and music are so perfectly married. She is, I think, at her best with the short lyrical poem or the song because in them the intensity of her ideas and feelings are expressed with most immediacy.

Although her view of the multiplicity and wonder of life is personal, she can yet be a remarkably objective, even astringent poet. She reminds one of Eliot's remark about "the impersonality of great poetry"; he added that to achieve this, a poet had to have a personality to start with.

Now and then Ruth Pitter undeniably touches greatness but she always captures our attention. Her belief in poetry as a way to understand things which reason cannot approach, the humour which forbids undue solemnity, the intensity and clarity of her perceptions are all shown well in the following two quotations; the first is humorous and taken from 'The Plain Facts by a Plain but Amiable Cat',

> See what a charming smile I bring
> Which no-one can resist;
> For I have found a wondrous thing –
> The Fact that I exist.

The second quotation comes from 'Fellow Creatures' which was written in 1938. It closes

> How shall the heart such rapture reach
> Till the stiff tongue its manners mend,
> To say to men, in human speech,
> Beloved, immortal spirit, friend?

ELIZABETH JENNINGS

MATERNAL LOVE TRIUMPHANT

or Song of the Virtuous Female Spider

Time was I had a tender heart,
But time hath proved its foe;
That tenderness did all depart,
And it is better so;
For if it tender did remain
How could I play my part,
That must so many young sustain?
Farewell the tender heart!

A swain had I, a loving swain,
A spider neat and trim,
Who used no little careful pain
To make me dote on him.
The fairest flies he brought to me,
And first I showed disdain;
For lofty we must ever be
To fix a loving swain.

But soon I bowed to nature's ends
And soon did wed my dear,
For all at last to nature bends;
So in a corner near
We fixed our web, and thought that love
For toil would make amends;
For so all creatures hope to prove
Who bow to nature's ends.

Ere long the sorry scrawny flies
For me could not suffice,
So I prepared with streaming eyes
My love to sacrifice.
I ate him, and could not but feel
That I had been most wise;
An hopeful mother needs a meal
Of better meat than flies.

My eggs I laid, and soon my young
Did from the same creep out:
Like little cupids there they hung
Or trundled round about;
And when alarmed, like a soft ball
They all together clung;
Ah mothers! we are paid for all
Who watch our pretty young.

For their sweet sake I do pursue
And slay whate'er I see;
Nothing's too much for me to do
To feed my progeny;
They'll do the same for me some day –
(Did someone say *Says You*?)
So still I leap upon the prey
And everything pursue.

Two bluebottles that loved so dear
Fell in my web together;
They prayed full fast and wept for fear,
But I cared not a feather;
Food I must have, and plenty too,
That would my darlings rear,
So, thanking Heaven, I killed and slew
The pair that loved so dear.

But most do I delight to kill
Those pretty silly things
That do themselves with nectar fill
And wag their painted wings;
For I above all folly hate
That vain and wasted skill
Which idle flowers would emulate;
And so the fools I kill.

Confess I may some virtue claim,
For all that I desire
Is first an honest matron's name,
Than which there is none higher;
And then my pretty children's good –
A wish that bears no blame;
These in my lonely widowhood
As virtues I may claim.

I look not here for my reward,
But recompense shall come
When from this toilsome life and hard
I seek a heavenly home;
Where in the mansions of the blest,
By earthly ills unmarred,
I'll meet again my Love, my best
And sole desired reward.

THE EARWIG'S COMPLAINT

being the history of his doleful case
miserably constrained to write ELEGY
that would fain sing Epithalamion

Armed Earwig I, that erst in prideful plight
Swanked in my mail and only swore by Mars;
Unlucky warrior and wretched wight,
That am dashed down to darkness from the stars!
Hear me, ye captains all! and vow the while
Your hearts to guard against the Cyprian's guile.

But one night since, the summer's long campaign
And bodeful frost constrained me to seek
Town-quarters from my tent upon the plain;
No palace, but some frugal inn; and eke
Some battens to recruit my weary breast,
And kind companions for a warrior's rest:

With snug dame Ladybird in scarlet brave
(Mine hostess kind) at chimney-cheek to chat:
To hear young Weevil squeak a sorry stave,
And kick his rump when he holds forth his hat;
Or, given full pots and cans, some little while
With old dan Spider's bloody brag beguile.

So led by chance (but grief doth cry Misled)
Up by a bowery jasmine did I scale
A lofty wall, and 'twixt delight and dread
I entered a wide chamber's secret pale;
There up a silken hanging did I glide,
Where it meseemed my wants might be supplied.

Yet much I feared the richness of the place,
Where how (said I) shall this ill-favoured weed,
This battered breastplate and this grisly face,
And (worse than all) these scanty ducats speed?
Yet on (quoth I), for I have earned a binge –
So reached the edge and tumbled off the fringe.

Soft on a damask mead I lighted straight;
No harm befallen; harm that might have saved!
Thence to an eminence, with wary gait,
I hied, o'er ground with great carnations paved;
And from the silken top with weary eye
Looked forth, and longed my lodging to espy.

But ah, the sight that did my gazes greet!
A goddess of celestial hue and size
Lay slumbering beneath a snowy sheet;
From the which spectacle my ravished eyes
Would not return, but on that heavenly she
Fastened instead, and owed no troth to me.

I but the bigness of three wheaten grains
And black withal, and she so great, so fair!
Whole continents of beauty, starry plains,
An universe of love surveyed I there!

24

And I will die, but I will share that sleep,
Madly I muttered, and within did creep:

And found myself within a heavenly vale
Whereof the ground was spread with living snow;
Or seemed as close inlaid with lilies pale
Heaved by a zephyr wandering to and fro;
Where, falling prone in an ecstatic swound,
I cried out Love! and kissed the enchanted ground.

It snatched my soul to those Elysian meads
Where on a day I shall dan Hector see
With nodding top and royal warrior's weeds
And visage terrible, yet sweet to me,
Cry, and bestow a brother captain's kiss,
Welcome, stout Earwig! to eternal bliss!

Ah, fatal boldness, woe, that I forgot
My steely casque, my greaves, my mailed arms,
Which to the silken blossoms of that spot
Did violence, and called forth loud alarms
As 'twere from underground, the mighty fair
Sending melodious thunders through the air!

There as I crouched in cold and awful dread
A most celestial hand of wondrous size
Plucked forth and cast me straightway out of bed,
Even to the floor, where I in woeful guise
Long time did lie sore bruised, and in my mind
Too sick to weep the heaven I left behind!

Ah, cruel goddess! do not queens delight
Warriors to honour, and their wounds to heal?
And am I then thus cast forth in despite
With insult sore, and hated every deal?
Most cruel, I continually say,
Who wouldst not crush but only cast away.

Come, death – come, kindly death, I straight would cry,
Take my dishonoured arms, lost cause, to thee;
But so say not, and I will tell you why;
Even for Earwig comfort there can be:
Lo! from beneath my mail I spread my wings!
And she – what knows she of such heavenly things?

LOVE'S MARTYRS

or The Bee Turned Anchorite

Like unto these immeasurable Mountains,
So is my painful Life, the burthen of ire:
For high be they, and high (was) my desire;
And I of Tears, and they are full of Fountains.
                                    Sir T. Wyatt

Our noble government and antique song,
Our glittering palaces lined and hung with gold;
Our various riches and ambrosial toil
I sing not here, but our heroic loves.
Venus, to whom our lives are dedicate,
Both the immortal sweetness and the sting,
Descend, and to this latter coldness lend
One tongue of flame, and so to heaven retire!

O virgin queen, that in the noon of May,
Radiantly apparelled, the sum of all things fair,
Like unto nought save godhead, issued forth
With us her train, her golden gentlemen!
We were love's college, Eros' servitors,
Who toiled not save in Auregina's praise,
Who vied in song and held a sole desire.
And yet, as from a cohort all attired
Alike, all armed in gold and plumed with fire,
All noble, mighty and magnanimous,
And all alike vowed to an holy cause,

One face pre-eminent, one more than man
Emerges, and one martial attitude
Makes of the mind a medal, struck for ever
With Honour's likeness not to be erased:
Even so the image of mine Astrophel[1]
Then did inform my soul, and fills it now.
I see thee, spirit blest, even as then,
Filled with love's rage and fire poetical,
Sail in our van, and on her sacred form
Anon bestow a sacrificial gaze,
Then to the fatal azure lift thy look,
And seem to breathe glory and tragedy.

But lo, she mounts! and so the hour is come
For which we all were nursed, and wherein all
Save one must be betrayed: that one elect
Triumph and die! she mounts, and straight is gone
From sight in the immortal ether, winged
With power of the whole nation she must bear.
Onward, pursue!...A moment's mutual gaze,
Then like a storm of meteors, reversed hail,
Or upward burst of fire, we follow her!

Beyond the roaring host that drove along
Through upper air, I marked mine empress far,
Where in the shining element the God
Himself appeared, and with sustaining hand
And fiery pinion urged her mighty way,
Hurling her through the concave: then anon
Turned to the rear his terrible regard
And with a smile that seemed to us a sword
Beckoned! and at the spur mine Astrophel
Shot from the ranks with more than mortal speed,
Devoured the gulf, and found both love and death.
I saw the God unstring his fatal bow
And melt into the sun; alas I saw
A star fell earthward, and mine own hope die.

[1] Pardon, sweet Sydney!

Ah, gentle noblemen, return again,
For you are cuckolds all; creep home, and be
Grateful while summer lasts for some small dole,
And at the frost be driven with female ire
And petty taunts beyond her shining doors:
Then like poor tavern-loiterers, broken men,
Awhile besiege with blundering gait the rose
Whose heart the rain hath rotted, and whose sweet
Juice is turned poison; whence soon sickening
And chilled in nipping nights, ye are no more,
And Boreas anon your relic wings
Whirls in cold corners with the wrack of leaves.
Not so for me! I marked where my king fell,
And on defeated vans I sank to him.
The dew had dashed him: 'twas a broken thing,
But fairest still: I delved a little grave,
Trembling with unused toil, and softly laid
The golden beauty in the silver sand:
Which done, in heaviness I lay along,
And like a traitor to my race blasphemed
Our female government, that murdered him
And wasted us: that solely bent on gain
Its myriad loveless drudges cherishes
And thrusts its murmuring poets forth to die.
And O for the last time I thought on her,
Now pressed upon by thronging household cares,
By teeming progeny, by hordes of slaves;
Alas, and to dire jealousy a prey:
Who raging inly ever and anon
Seeks the pearled domes where the supplantress lurks,
Thirsting implacably to shed the blood
Of royal virgins; by obsequious
Yet resolved minions' hands hardly restrained.
Sad transformation from godlike maid
To murderous matron and to plotting queen!
Hard thought, at which mine eyes now drop anew.

Who'll bargain with a broken gentleman?
Come, who will chaffer for these costly tears,
Mine only treasure? I have fetched them far,
Even from heaven and hell, and have spent all,
And in my tattered tawny velvet stand
Here in the chilly eve and proffer them.
Who lacks a gaud? who'll buy, that I may rear
With but the price of one a sepulchre
Well worthy of mine Astrophel and me?
Give me but half its worth, I could purvey
The weeping Graces and the mourning Loves,
And for the midst a sad Calliope
All glimmering alabaster; could make write
Love's Martyrs on the basis, and contrive
Some curious fountain for the Muse's tears.
But there is none to buy; the orient drops
Sink into earth, ah less esteemed than rain,
Ungrateful to these meanest herbs, my bed;
Unseen of all save surly Vespa, who
On her mechanic solitary way
Ranges the melancholy wilderness,
Too dull even to cry *What make you here?*

The enchanter's nightshade and rough bramble-rose
Must yield my food, and this dank covert be
My roof till I am sped, and my fair hope
Him and Parnassus; they who therein dwell
Have loved our race, and are hospitable,
Nor will deny some pasture in the thyme
To us by death and desolation tried,
By love afflicted, by affection bound,
And not unskilled in song. Thither I go
To meet him in the purple, and to hear
As if the golden age were come again,
Blind majesty still singing to the Bee,
Homer and Astrophel in antiphon.

RESURGAM

or the glorious and pitiful history of the
HERETICAL CATERPILLAR

Hearken my strange and sad calamity,
Fair gentles that in bliss shall come to dwell;
And look you lose not the analogy
Which shall unfold as I the story tell:
For I have inklings both of heaven and hell,
And see most strangely, as your poets do,
Truth lurking in the bottom of the well;
I have rejoiced and I have suffered too,
And now must end my days in mickle wrath and rue.

I a soft worm, as you have often seen,
Upon a cabbage found my daily fare:
But not the commonest, it was not green,
But of a tincture wonderful and rare;
Purple it was, as robes that monarchs wear,
Being of the costlier or pickling kind;
And cast abroad upon the amorous air
A great effulgence, wherein you may find
The means whereby my soul to lofty themes inclined.

There, sleeping in its brave ensanguined heart,
Wrapped in that noble colour, virtue's sign,
There 'gan within my ravished spirit start
Strange visions of felicity divine:
And this poor greenish faintheart blood of mine
Was warmed into a tide of rushing bliss;
A boundless sea of purple-cabbage wine,
Which wave on wave of wafting harmonies
Rolled, until I was rapt to where all rapture is.

Methought I saw a wingèd creature fly
That seemed most nearly of the Cherubim:
His pinions white with many a dusky eye
And dainty down on every part of him;

30

Noble he was in every lightsome limb;
He scorned to browse upon the herbage dun,
But of the flowers which in his light were dim
Sipped wantonly and tasted one by one;
Then at my side sat down and glistened in the sun.

O beauty (then said I) whence are you born?
What shining cradle by the springs of day
Hath lost that loveliness, which puts to scorn
All that doth creep or on a cabbage prey?
For so your fairness doth my soul betray,
That having seen I covet only death;
Do long most strangely to be snatched away,
Yea, hurried from my being in a breath,
Ere the brave wings are spread, the vision vanisheth!

Brother (said he, which did most strangely sound)
Dear brother, be content, for thou shalt be
Even as I, and shun the sickly ground,
Shalt suck on sweetness and live royally;
Yea, greater good than wings and sweetness see,
For thou shalt love thy lovely counterpart;
Shalt mount the summit of felicity
And live more greatly in another's heart,
Translated from the greedy worm which now thou art.

I tell thee true that fair Imago am,
Death lies not in your coffin-chrysalid,
But merrier life and love that knows no shame
Are in that curious tomb or cradle hid:
Think then on this when desolate amid
Terror of failing life and fears of hell;
Say then thy loud RESURGAM and be rid
Of these strong nothings; then bethink thee well
Of the unprisoned soul that did the tidings tell.

Straight I awoke and to the light crept forth,
Still in my joy, and yet misdoubting much
The Vision as a thing of little worth,
A mocking dream, the old poetic touch!
Yet as I crawled from out my purple hutch
Behold mine angel of the air again,
Like a loud hymn of heavenly triumph, such
As men may write in most celestial strain
In characters of gold on skins of Tyrian grain!

On Tyrian skins the characters of gold!
Who would not die the death, or walk in fire,
Who thus might see upon the air unfold
The signed sealed charter of his one desire?
Methought I heard on high an heavenly choir,
Whose lofty numbers flowing forth to form
An orbèd triumph, struck the plangent lyre
Of the arched firmament, and with a storm
Of awful music cried aloud Behold the Worm!

My sense regained, I sought the glutton band
Of my green brethren at their long repast,
Feeling myself elect and ordinand
To an high-priesthood, to a kingship chaste,
Well fit to be their head, as having cast
All but one skin of sad mortality:
And this my wondrous history in haste
I did rehearse; but these most swinishly
But guzzled ravening on and paid no heed to me.

So from the place of mine unworthy peers
I straight departed, shaking off the dust,
And poured my tale into the tender ears
Of the new-hatched, who with an eager gust
Devoured the story; such did prove the trust
Of these worm-innocents, that nought would do
But to the purple cabbage go they must:
Thereon would live, that they might prove anew
The lovely legend, and perchance Imago view.

There I abode awhile with them in joy,
There did Imago light and talked with them:
In which delight was found no base alloy,
But each felt on his brow a diadem
Thickset with many an immortal gem;
But better priest than parent did I prove,
For these that should have gnawed both leaf and stem
Forgot their commons out of very love,
Sat still as marble stones and fixed their gaze above.

Which scandal was not hidden overlong,
For on a day a fat and busy knave,
A worm full greedy, with an evil tongue,
Walked in on us, snug in our purple cave,
And his most base opinion loudly gave
That worms, especially the young, should take
No care for anything beyond the grave;
And me he called a windy purple fake,
Nor stayed to cull his words for innocence's sake.

Worms be engendered (belched the blustering beast)
From humorous ichors by the sun his heat;
Their piety and only interest
Should be to eat and eat and still to eat:
Yea, lie upon and grovel in their meat,
Cast skin on skin, and wax surpassing fat:
Nor curious boons of heaven to entreat,
Even as I hear of this mad autocrat;
But bravely gorge, then cease; and that (said he) is that.

Throughout mine heart it struck a deadly cold,
To hear this world his voice so loud proclaim
Such perfect beastliness with visage bold,
Approve himself and glory in the same;
Which fair Imago's loves did so defame
That all the world about me red I saw,
And though for priests to fight is counted shame,
Aloud I cried, Silence, thou ugly maw,
Thou rumbling belly, peace! and biffed him on the jaw.

33

What sad confusion thereon did ensue,
Or how my bantlings all in terror flying
Left me forlorn, I will not tell to you,
But pass it swiftly; presently a crying
Arose without, which clamour not defying
I went to meet; the mob with one assent
Cried Take the traitor, hang him for his lying;
Then haled me forth on bloody vengeance bent,
And me till I should die in mouldy crevice pent.

Here as I lie I hear the busy tongue
Of trollop Rumour tell the miseries
Which now befall those undirected young,
Strangely abused by grief and fantasies:
How one to feed on flowery nectar tries,
Gnaws at the blossoms and is much upset;
And one would sail as fair Imago flies,
Leaps from a tree and pays his folly's debt
With broken neck, at which hard news mine eyes are wet.

And one poor innocent my prison passed,
Wandering distractedly in frenzy frantic;
Anon rehearsing, brokenly and fast,
A little creed which vanity pedantic
Moved me to make for them; with gesture antic
Anon his little claspers to the sky
Stretched in despair; then leaping corybantic
Cried with a crazy shriek Behold I fly!
Then sank to earth, and at each spiracle did sigh.

Unhappy Curlicue, my scholar dear!
Out of my love I did but seek to teach
Thee of thy blessed lot in heavenly sphere;
Alas! I have but made a fatal breach
In thy green intellects, which could not reach
So lofty theme, and so thou art betrayed;
And thee and thy fair likeness each to each
Shall never fly, nor be Imago made;
But without hope of resurrection seek the shade.

Seek the deep shade the where I soon shall be!
For much I fear that fell Ichneumon thrust
Her treacherous egg and greedy spawn in me,
And made a Poet, full of sickly lust;
Too delicate to do as others must,
Doting on heaven since his life is hell,
And sinking hopeless down into the dust,
There to become a rotten empty shell
Without a soul, because in him the Pest doth dwell.

Yet peace is mine; I dreamed another dream,
Unlike the first, full of a sober grace,
A calm beyond despair, as when the beam
Oft the full moon illumes the water's face:
Methought appeared to me in this sad place
A thick short Man, crabbed visage, gnarly head,
And looks which did my little griefs efface;
In whose crisped scanty locks as in a bed
Lay lurking Curlicue, unfelt but comforted.

Ah, fellow worm (then said that worthy wight),
I was condemned, my fault was like to thine:
Corruption of the young, and high despite
Against those things my fellows held divine;
Like thee I did in mouldy prison pine;
I died, thou diest, and our histories
Remain, a warning and an anodyne:
But there are heavens beyond heavens; these
Be but the ghostly Shadows of the Images.

FAREWELL TO BEAUTY

Archangel at dawn,
angel in the morning,
lost at noon, ah lost in labour,
lost when the forest was forsaken
for the field too often ploughed –
would you had been lost for ever,
obscene when rediscovered!
How dare you
so blasphemously reappear
as a kind of auntie mabel
o god auntie mabel
sitting under the rambler roses
tinkle tinkle yowl
pinky panky rambler roses
panky punky dorothy perkins
in your libertyhat
and guineahen foulard?
Flaccid breasted in your shower-of-mud foulard!!!

Awareness horribly agile
wide-eyed wonder sharp-horned terror
leap from you snorting
goodbye auntie dear
sweet of you to have me
its been just lovely but
I MUST FLY
fly before I see
the ultimate corruption,
fly before I hear
what I know, ah what I know.

DIGDOG

*Inspired by the English of a Belgian hotel-keeper. "Ze ladies,
zey lof ze Griffon Bruxellois; mais moi, je préfére ze English
digdog! ze brave renardearther." i.e. fox-terrier.*

Rooting in packingcase of
dirty straw hurling
lumps of it overboard moaning desire
moaning desire of vermin lovely rat
ineffable mouse attar of felicity
BUT there is nothing
nothing but dirt and darkness
but strawdirt chaffdust smellillusion ALAS.
BRAVE CHIEN ANGLAIS
NOBLE RENARDEARTHER
DIGDOG

Alas I also
root in earth desiring
something for nothing digging down to peace.
Follow the mole and not the lark
bet with the bloke who knows
peace lies there whence from the dark
arise the lily and the rose,
peace rains down in rivers of gold
and there great nuggets of sleep
wait for the seeker ever been sold
sit on your tail and weep
for there is nothing
nothing but dust and darkness
but strawdirt chaffdust smellillusion ALAS.
LACHE ESPRIT ANGLAIS
POLTRON DE RENARDEARTHER
DIGDOG

PORTRAIT OF A GENTLEMAN

in business for himself in a small way and not doing too well owing
to trade depression and want of low qualities

At the spraygun stands large heroic Ted.
The screech of air, the thunder of the fan
Beat in huge billows of din about his head
But can affect no feature of the Man,
Who thinks "This blasted stuff does go on thin",
But looks – this is your cue, I think, Miss Muse,
Mount the compressed-air cylinder, and begin.
She from that vibrant rostrum frankly views
The face, the attitude, the matchless thews –
She from all little loves and passions free –
And opens thus. O godlike Ted! I see
On thy great breast the brazen harness glow,
On thy great shins behold the shining greaves,
Above thy countenance see the red plume blow,
The helm invisible, the sacred leaves.
Captain of all lost causes, and the head
Of fallen enterprise, I see thee stand
Like Alexander summoning his dead
Warriors about him in the spectral land.
Ah, should times mend, my Edward! thou wouldst fall
To sad vulgarity a sudden prey;
I see the Residence, the Car, and all
Thy wife's long dreams come true in dread array.
But ere the moment passes, let me say:
Ted in hard times is beautiful; he seems
Like Agamemnon, like the bird of Jove,
Like the great golden navy of my dreams
Manned by dear virtue and unbent by love,
Trampling down briny trouble; O that straight
We might beyond the raging of our fate
Cast anchor in the unimagined streams!

TIMELIE TYDINGES FOR LOUELES LADYES

(& look ye miss not ye speciall offere)

*No prize is offered for indicating the defects
either of the O.E. Allit, or the period English.*

Ladyes that ben nat louesome & crien wel a wey
Hearken how ye mought be heled & that in ful hast,
Crien wel a wey namo but woxen right mirie,
Bi an herbe that I haue bi loue of ye seyntes
Got bi grete conyng vpon a blissid tyde
Springand ful swetelie bisyde o welle springe.
Bote for that my manere smelleth of ye molde
Hearkneth & heareth nowe this wonder wight,
List to o ladye ye louesomest of alle
Lionor that hight, and shenteth not my speche,
Bote listneth ful lowlie, lightsom to be made.
Seth ye ladye Lionor, Louesome ne was I neuer,
Tyme was I was ful foule & blak as anie crowe.
Manie maydens thereof made them grete mirthe
That ye fiende was my fader & mudd my moderes name.
I mourned in ye morninge ne mirie was bi nyghte,
Marrd all my maydenhoode & made al manere wo.
Bote on a daye as I went & wandered in ye toune,
Bi a blissid hap, *a benedicite,*
At a boothe did bugge ye hope of mine hele
Of that worthie wight this wonder wede that selleth,
To eten thereof & crie wel a wey namo.
Nowe hale is myn hew & hole is myn harte,
I caste away care & caryll ful clere,
Kirte vppe my cote & lepe forth lite.
Four knyghtes of my fairness ben fond & eke fayne,
Gramercye me crieth & gruccheth one to other.
Wherefore I rede al ladyes of ye lond
That they eten of ye herbe & conneth so theyre doghteres,
Then schall they showe ful schene ne think ye none othere.
Nowe lieveth on this ladye, ye brightest bird in boure,
Seeketh myn hous in ye yerde of seynt Poules,
And for that ye toun of ladyes doth lacke

That bene to straunge strondes ygon & holie schrines,
Ye schalle haue of ye herbe for o poure penie
Enogh & to spare, & nede namo to bugg;
But and if ye quene & ye corte com home
Good hap schall yt be if ye gett for a grote
Ye fagott that a ferthyng schall fecche yow this daye;
And that ful drie & drere if anie to be hadd.
Further, if ye seke me when I be nat bisie,
I schalle shew yow in a boke, methinke of Aristotil,
That telleth & techeth ye wonder of ye wede,
Seth that it ben of Venus verilie
Of al herbes ye highest bote hard to be hadd.
Ye are to seke an hous at ye sign of ye Serpent,
The which when yow haue founde ye maye ye bettere knowe
For that att ye windowe sitteth att hys werke
Perkyn my prentis a ful fayre freke
With a watchett courtepie & hose of ye same,
That looketh aye for ladyes & crieth when they come.
And nowe to ye sauing loue of alle ye seyntes
I commende alle louseom both sympel & gente,
Come hithere in al hast with penie ynn your hond.

                                                    (Advert).

FOWLS CELESTIAL AND TERRESTRIAL

or The Angels of the Mind

The watery swan

Where dost thou feed?
In the river-slime and weed.
Where hatch thy young?
The dank marish-reeds among.
Art thou at peace?
Nay, for I fear my enemies.
What dost thou then?
I run full fierce at dogs and men.

What feet are those?
Black webs to go where water flows.
What fair long neck?
At the dark bottom food to seek.
What broad white pens?
To sail over stagnant fens.
Alas, then tell how it may be
Thou shinest so well in poesy?

Ah, then she bridled up her lordly head,
Spread forth her silver plume in clean array,
Arched her queenly neck, and with her red
And polished bill down her sleek sides made play:
Waxed on a sudden brighter than the day,
And so lift up on me a different eye,
Oared from the brink like a brave ship away,
Then from the lily-isle where she did lie
Spoke while the enchanted water lapsed in music by.

All elegy am I and martyrdom,
The sailing song's alternate ebb and flow;
To some high aspiration and to some
Still chastity that clothed herself in snow:
In the mind's heaven I like an angel go
Down a most silent stream, imagining
Like Narcis that I see my love below;
And mute I am until that death shall bring
A voice and then that love unspeakable I sing.

The Nightingale that nests on Earth

What doest thou all day?
Catch grubs and flies where e'er I may.
And fed, what then?
Do as befits an honest hen.
Thy nest where found?
In ferny thickets on the ground.
Thy greatest care?
That my three nestlings well may fare.

41

Lov'st thou so sore?
As other birds do and no more.
Why then so sing?
'Tis but love's madness in the spring.
Alas, is this that paragon
Of sadness poets dote upon?

Even as I spoke it was already night;
The homespun bird took wing, was no more seen,
But peerless notes of sorrowful delight
Dropped down like pearls the leafy boughs between:
The mourning of an ill-entreated queen
Of murdered innocence with woe complained,
Then sobbing with a muted and serene
Sound, the poor soul with godly voice sustained
Her breaking heart, and with her faith her heaven regained.

I am that Philomel, whose bitter shame
Is wrought to royal song (said she with tears);
Ill was my fortune, worthy is my fame,
Whence all unhappy poets are my peers:
The luckless lover in my ditty hears
His woes adorned with rarest elegy;
It seems his hurt is healed through his ears;
And so for ever in the company
Of the mind's angels not the least angelic I.

The Bird of Paradise, airy, as inhabiting the Lofty Trees

Art thou a Bird,
Or idle legend I have heard;
Liv'st thou indeed?
In Indian forest do I breed.
A heavenly place?
Some beauties, much that is most base.
What is thy good?
Like thine, my mate, my nest and food.
Thy greatest ill?
The naked Indian would me kill.

Thy voice is sweet?
Merely the peacock's counterfeit.
Whence then thy name?
My fair attire is all my fame.
〜Alas, I thought that thou didst sing
In heaven, and find it no such thing.

She clapped her blinding wings and straight up flew
To the high summit of a cedar green:
A beam of dazzling silver from the blue
Lighted on her, that now was no more seen
As earthly fowl, but even as she had been
One of the awful burning cherubim;
Upon a fiery cloud her breast did lean,
With heaven-assaulting gaze she pierced the dim
Azure, and *holy, holy, holy,* was her hymn.

High is the battlement of heaven, but high
My range, and I to heaven can attain.
I leave below the summits of the sky,
The cloud doth stretch beneath me as a plain:
Still, still I soar, and rest not till I gain
The gates of an whole pearl, the golden floor:
Then in that tree of which I am most fain
I light, where of all bliss is endless store:
There sing beside my shining mate for evermore.

The Phoenix, called of Arabia Felix

Where may I find
Thee? Only in the aspiring mind.
Where is thy nest?
If thou liv'st truly, in thy breast.
Nowhere on earth?
My death is secret and my birth.
What is thy food?
A fire that burns in solitude,
In the which flame
I mine own child and parent am.

Fair on the incense-hill, her precious pyre,
She sat, and royally her royal crest
Reared up, all crowned as with eternal fire:
Like an immortal martyr richly dressed
In an embalming flame, to manifest
How well her deathless soul can bear, how long,
The cruel element that burns her breast:
Then from these odours and these flames among
Proceeded as by miracle her silent song.

This mortal must her immortality
Put on, and this corruptible be made
To that which shall not perish (thus said she),
Must with a heavenly body be arrayed:
How then shall grisly death make me afraid?
Behold how I from mine own ashes rise,
Bloom in the fire where lately I did fade,
And newly-minted from the sacrifice
Greet the no-brighter sun with young rejoicing eyes.

So ever sing, dear angels of the mind!
Thou, chantress by the waters desolate,
And thou who dost in the dark greenwood find
Love's pain made perfect, and a sorry fate
The source of a high song; and thou, the gate
Of heaven that assaultest, and dost see
Lodged in the tree of life thy happy mate;
And thou, the voice of immortality,
Sole in thy secret dwelling, fairest Piety!

THE PIOUS LADY TROUT

Arrayed in golden beauty, silver light,
Stuck with gay rubies, veiled in azure sheen,
Sidling among the wonderful and bright
Weeds, and the fair white stones that shine between,
I to delight and to all honour bred
Rejoice in a resplendent ladyhead.

Clean is the aureate gravel where I lie,
Clear is this stream, and as I go I see
Rare groves reflected, and a nether sky
That smileth upward, decked full tenderly
With rosy cloud, save where on high the swan
Like a most princely ship comes oaring on.

The water-ousel, wimpled as with lawn,
On weedy stone works like a busy nun,
The vole toward her granary withdrawn
Steers with her grass-seed, dressed in habit dun;
Dull elves and homespun toilers! while I shine
At ease, and grace this garden crystalline.

But if my place and tender body show
So fair, how fair must be my heavenly soul!
These lovely gauds are my desert below,
But Providence hath destined me the whole
Large kingdom and gay court of Paradise,
Meet for a lady beautiful and wise.

How am I fed? most fitly on the fair
Stream's self, but I myself a task have set
To leap and snatch those sinners of the air
That off this element presume to get;
So piously I purge the gentle sky
Of nasty atomies that dare to fly.

THE MAYFLY

Love me but once I say,
For once sufficeth;
I sink at close of day,
The next one riseth.
Behold me where I go,
Lost if you stay me not;
I am a breath, and so
Love and delay me not.

Some splashing undergrad
Engulfs my neighbour;
Yon greedy trout hath had
Ten with no labour.
A speedy death I see
Below and above me,
The only remedy
Is that you love me.

I the day's beauty am
And the night's sorrow
From the dark deep I came
And go to-morrow.
Love me while yet I shine
In my best feather,
And for grief's anodyne
We'll die together.

THE FROG IN THE WELL

A True History, and Image of the State

From the far brink of sacred Helicon
Stoop, kindly Muse, to hymn the tale of one
Poor atomy, whose tragedy was wrought
To comedy by means she never sought,
Nor could have known; ah let me then believe
In saving fates, and hope when most I grieve.

Some rustic boys set forth in bloomy spring
To fish for tadpoles: pendent from a string
An urn they bore which erst had jam contained;
Long did they strive, and of bad sport complained;
One only wriggler did their search reward,
The season then fast settling summerward.
Then homeward straggling, on a mighty tea
Resolved, and much desiring to be free
From the loathed vessel's all but barren weight,
They to a horrid and a lingering fate
Consigned the victim; thoughtlessness more fell
Than crime deliberate! In a lonely well
They chucked the jar with its imprisoned nymph
Down through the darkness to the icy lymph.

Ah poor Sabrina! what unknown despair
Clutched at thine heart, sunk in deep prison, where
No food appeared in those pure waters cold,
Nor any blade of grass you watched unfold;
Where scarce a ray of light to thee could drop,
For a stout hatch secured the domy top!
Some few poor ferns she saw with hopeless love
Glimmer in ghostly greenness far above;
Her sole relief from the engulfing tide
To cling at whiles to the rough bricky side.
Not long she lived, say you? you do not know
How long a reptile may unnourished go.
Summer was spent, the autumn almost come,

And she still pent in the relentless tomb;
Her metamorphosis she even achieved,
A smaller frog than you would have believed
Had you not seen; but the flat wistful head
Grew to full size, so we must think she fed,
Though upon what, and on how little too,
We marvel much, and much the same must rue:
And pity muses how that little brain
Wove stratagems the distant top to gain;
How those frail midget-hands have striven to scale
The tyrant wall, for ever doomed to fail:
Thinks of those pretty eyes still fixed on high
In huge despair unknown to passers-by.

Till on a fateful day of August heat
The tempest gathered, and the lightnings fleet
Flew o'er the welkin, while a hollow boom
Of thunder shook the water of her tomb:
Down from the pregnant sky the fluid teemed,
The runnels roared and all the meadows steamed;
Nor was it long before the porous sides
Of the well dripped, and all the stealthy tides
Of the field-drainage swelled the scanty spring,
And hope grew strong in the imprisoned thing.
Still, still the flood mounts with resistless urge
And now is but a foot below the verge.

Fast to a twig she clung, that many a day
Had mouldered in the nether floods away,   ·
And scarce her eyes or her weak heart could bear
Light, and deliverance now come so near.
The hatch remained, but she'd admit no doubt
That some kind chink therein would let her out:
Let her but grasp the edge, she'd starve to death,
Or till grown spare enough to slip beneath.
She measured in a hopeful agony
The few top inches still remaining dry:
When the blind heaven its saving tears allayed,
The trickle ceased, and straight the tide was stayed,

48

And slowly downward from the mocking brink
She with her rotten twig began to sink.
Poor soul! I cannot sing the pains of hell,
And so that last defeat may never tell.

Now for thy faith! still call on heaven to save,
And save it shall, though every demon rave.
The hatch is lifted and a human face
Looks down into the dim and dismal place:
The human vision sees the victim there,
And human reason knows her whole despair.
A tactful hand (no paw of murderous lout,
But kind Ruth Pitter's) plucks the sufferer out,
And to a pond where she may soon be fat
She takes the wizen creature in her hat;
And many a balmy tear the bard doth shed
On the mere tadpole with the full-grown head:
Perchance some simile therein she sees,
Or sure would not waste brine on things like these.
Yet, ah believe that if the fates can do
Thus for a frog, we may be hopeful too
That we shall see this wretched State of ours
Snatched from the malice of the nether powers!

THE COFFIN-WORM

which consider

The Worm unto his love: lo, here's fresh store;
Want irks us less as men are pinched the more.
Why dost thou lag? thou pitiest the man?
Fall to, the while I teach thee what I can.
Men in their lives full solitary be:
We are their last and kindest company.
Lo, where care's claws have been! those marks are grim;
Go, gentle Love, erase the scar from him.

Hapless perchance in love (most men are so),
Our quaint felicity he could not know:
We and our generation shall sow love
Throughout that frame he was not master of;
Flatter his wishful beauties; in his ear
Whisper he is at last beloved here;
Sing him (and in no false and siren strain)
We will not leave him while a shred remain
On his sweet bones: then shall our labour cease,
And the imperishable part find peace
Even from love; meanwhile how blest he lies,
Love in his heart, his empty hands, his eyes.

A TROPHY OF ARMS

The primrose awakens, but
I lean here alone
Where the proud helmet is cut
In the hard stone:
Where the true sword is hung
With the straight spear,
When all is said and sung
My heart is here.

A nameless tomb I guard,
I know not for whose sake,
Nor for what far reward;
Yet I hear wake
The voice of honour, calling
From the bones I have cherished:
"The mighty are not fallen,
Nor the weapons of war perished."

SIMILE

Like a song that shall be heard
Long after any singing bird:
Like a tune that shall resound
When pipes are broken, tabors burned,
And all the minstrels under ground:
Like a voice divinely turned,
Falling, falling through the air
When there are no more planets there
And space and purity are bare:
That shall lift and sing and fly
And light on summits of the sky,
On bodiless summits of no time;
And in the sea of ether swim,
And on light alone shall climb,
A naked and a shining hymn:
Like the triumph in the ways
Of heaven on high holidays,

Is a thing all men may see
In a short life times two or three –
A look of steadfast constancy.

AN IMPATIENCE

Great men and learned I can hate,
And would confound them if I could:
I saw a simple thing of late,
A soul that lived in solitude.

In anger have I closed the book
That lusts to make all men believe:
But the lone wildling creature's look
Homage demands and shall receive.

Your thoughts are vast, yet shapeless things,
And never done, like Babel tower:
But to its life this spirit brings
Completeness, like the five-leaved flower.

You end in chaos, as you began;
You are made filth and food of flies:
This loves, and when it ends its span,
As flowers fall, even so it dies.

Your way, your ends are dread to me,
When in your hell I share your dream:
But when this dies, I seem to see
Five petals on the sliding stream.

THE ETERNAL IMAGE

Her angel looked upon God's face
As eagles gaze upon the sun,
Fair in the everlasting place.

And saw that everything is one
And moveless, in the eternal light:
Never completed, not begun.

She on the earth, with steadfast sight,
Stood like an image of the Muse
Amid the falling veils of night:

Her feet were silvered in the dews,
Dew fell upon her darkling tree,
And washed the plain with whitish hues.

Standing so still, what does she see?
She sees the changeless creature shine
Apparelled in eternity:

She knows the constancy divine;
The whole of life sees harvested,
And frozen into crystalline

And final form, the quick, the dead,
All that has ever seemed to change,
Possess at once the pale and red:

All that from birth to death may range
Newborn and dead she sees, nor says
The vision to be sad or strange.

How may this serve her mortal ways?
Truly it cannot buy her bread
Nor ease the labour of her days:

But calm her waking, quiet her bed,
For she has seen the perfect round
That binds the infant to the dead,

And one by one draws underground
All men; and still, and one by one,
Into the air the living bound,

Never completed, not begun.
With burning hair, with moveless grace,
As eagles gaze against the sun

Her angel looks upon God's face.

THE COMET

O still withhold thyself, be not possessed:
Hyperbola, the dread uncharted line,
Debase not into orbit; still make shine
Portentous rays of arrowy unrest

Among the earthy planets. Know not law,
Here are too many who lie straitly bound:
Fly all but in the sun, and shooting round
Dart to the outer darkness of our awe:
And if there be incalculable return,
Come in another shape with monstrous hair
Or triple train enclosing half the skies:
Still let thy face with various omens burn,
Still shun the reasoned pathways to despair,
Nor answerable be to earthly eyes.

ON A PASSAGE FROM THE *METAMORPHOSES*

No wreath of heavy-seeded sesame,
No cake of bread nor jar of funeral wine
For Baucis and Philemon. Here her tree,
Mingling its boughs with his, still fronts the shine
Of the broad east, marks the faint day decline,
And over olive-silver still may see
The moon through many a gleam and shadow flee.

I doubt not they were buxom, that their brows
Took the full sun and browned like leaves at fall,
Nor that they tried the temper of their vows
With words, or else were human not at all:
But now as Oak and Elm they are so tall
That their companionship is godlike grown;
With strong roots anchored on the rocks of hell
And highest leaves abroad in heaven blown,
With Baucis and Philemon it is well.

Lo, web on silver web time overlays
Upon simplicity, and with much gold
Ancient remembrance hangs their homely ways;
Fame purples all the fleeces in their fold;
Yet I doubt not they thought themselves too bold

In bidding that strange majesty to meat;
Though a Philosopher the man might seem,
Awful he lightened, and the Other's feet
Moved as a faun's move in some forest dream.

This I make theirs; the wellspring in the north,
With northern elder and with grass more deep
Than in their land; water that flows not forth,
But pent in fern and darkness still doth keep
A faithfulness, love not forgotten in sleep:
Not like the market-going brooks that trace
Their course by gossip reeds, but as the dews
That make a silver twilight in this place,
And bathe the white feet of the wandering Muse
In windless hollows where such spirits use.

For I have not walked Phrygia, ancient pair,
Father Philemon, mother Baucis kind:
Turbulent heavens and still-freezing air,
The sad eternal rain, the south-west wind,
Flails of hard sleet and hail, and sea-fogs blind
Compass me wholly, so that still I crave
Rest underneath your boughs, and in the sun
Forgetfulness of voice of hollow wave,
And of the sea and sky all grey and dun,
And of the sea-fowl sorrowful every one.

Yet under English elm and the loved oak
In thought a faint felicity is mine:
I hear the hospitality you spoke,
Hear from the skin the gladly-given wine
Leap zealously to serve the lips divine:
Or is it but the cold spring's quiet song
Rising through fragrance of the fallen leaves?
Not so, but murmurs in an ancient tongue
From gods and men at peace, and swallows in the eaves.

HEROIC COUPLETS

I thank Almighty God, who gave to me
Nothing and none to envy, save these three:
The man who rides good horses: he that can
Sail his own ship, the very Englishman:
And that most blessed man, who calls his own
Some little manor-house of brick or stone,
Or fairest oak and plaster, nobly reared
When Bess was deified, and Philip feared.
O the sweet havens with their terraces,
Old gardens, sunken lawns, and singing trees:
With fretted chimneys flowering in smoke
Of airy blue from fragrant English oak,
In whose loved smell there lives the history
Of the whole woodland, and the happy tree;
His leaves, his nutty mast, his lichened bark,
His image in the pool most clear and dark,
The primroses that smile about his foot,
And the wild brake that shades the gnarly root:
The stag that frets his fevered poll in spring
On the rough rind, and the great swine that bring
Such tumult to their banquet in the fall;
A Bacchus' rout beneath the umbrage tall.
Not only silvan mirth in smoke I see,
But heavenly grace of hospitality;
The waxen light, the ancient tankards' gleam,
And still affection dearer than a dream.
There with brave oak the inner walls are fine,
On which the children's cowslip-tresses shine,
Or neighbours' wiser silver, much more fair
Than heirloom gold, howbeit old or rare.
Much could I say of lovely lavender,
Where the bees make such business and burr,
Of the warm walls where aged apricots
Drop their too heavy wealth on marjoram-plots,
And classic walnut, the repast of Jove,
Spreads fruit on earth and shining shade above;
Of roses, cabbage, damask, moss and musk,

And cloves so buxom that they burst the husk,
And all the sweets the happy manors know
From the first snowdrop to the latest snow;
So many, a man for luxury might faint,
Or wiser, weep for thanks, and turn a saint.
But on no further beauty will I glance,
Lest I my poverty and ignorance
Should too much hate; that must I shun and flee,
Since these by Heaven were sent to live with me.
Cheerly, child Ignorance; I meant no harm
In praising seats that look so fair and warm;
And if thou wert not by my side, I dare
Roundly affirm they would not look so fair.
And thou dear Poverty, blest by word divine,
For no sweet Manor thou and I shall twine:
Or only when thou drop'st thy daisy-wreath
And tear, into my sepulchre beneath;
The dusty daisies from the roadside waste,
And the brave tear, the only gems thou hast.
Then must we part, my dears! when I shall go
To a brave Mansion ye can never know.

GENTLE JOY

Sing, gentle joy, naught can betray thee;
Neither our sinning nor our sorrow
Can in thy sprightly going stay thee;
Our day is darkness, and our morrow
Is death; yet still the note thou ringest
Lifts up the spirit as thou singest.

Tears are no majesty, and sighing
Like an east wind, a blight unholy:
Death has no crown, for all are dying,
None is admired for melancholy;
Yet single as the daystar burneth
The heart to which its Joy returneth!

We rise and pass, but still thou stayest,
And like the sun returnest ever:
Thou canst not die, and never mayest
From Paradise thyself dissever:
Thou risest; all is cured, forgiven:
Joy is on earth, and earth is heaven.

FOR SLEEP, OR DEATH

Cure me with quietness,
Bless me with peace;
Comfort my heaviness,
Stay me with ease.
Stillness in solitude
Send down like dew;
Mine armour of fortitude
Piece and make new:
That when I rise again
I may shine bright
As the sky after rain,
Day after night.

DEAR PERFECTION

In the least flowering weed she lies,
Those buds are eyes,
Those leaves are hands, that little stem
Body and arms that flourish them;
That seed's a crown;
Those dews are tears that tremble down.

That look is hers, the attitude,
The solitude:
The dear simplicity suffices,

Shaming the sum of my devices;
See how she prays,
Speaketh, and sings in divers ways.

Sometimes I see her smile in men;
The impotent pen
Craves to be broken, and the mind
Never the noble word can find
To sing their state
Or their most worth to celebrate.

I can but say that I have seen
Her beauty clean
Shine in the humble, and her grace
Look from simplicity's own face:
Then do I smile
And sigh for very love the while.

There is a place where she must be
A deity:
There on a day she'll bid me tell
These that I loved them very well;
But now I keep
Silence, and bid my love go sleep.

But here's where she is wholly mine:
Up from the line
Of lovely verse she leaps, and takes
In her strong hand my soul that shakes,
That faints and dies,
Yet lives by looking in her eyes.

Dearest Perfection! let me be
A spark of thee;
Light my small taper at thy fire
And live a flame of pure desire:
Shine like the sun,
Burn like the Phoenix, which is one.

STORM

I have seen daylight turn cadaverous,
And on the earth the fixed defeated look,
The grim north light, as on the face of the dead
Reflected up from the wan-shining sea
Where they put forth utterly desolate;
Often have seen the hideous face of storm,
All in a moment changing balefully
Wholesome to fell, and homeliest to strange:
A yellow awe and a swift pestilence
Precipitating natural decays:
Till from the quarter of the awaited woe
Bows the whole landscape in a fleeing arc,
Heads, treetops, cornfields, all to leeward strain:
A billow heaped of the whole atmosphere,
A shriek that snatches at complete revenge,
Hurled like an airy war across the world,
Level the fields that shall not rise again,
And opening all the gates of upper flood,
Drown, blast and splinter, thunder above and below.

Have I not seen the sudden storm in the mind,
Conceived of anguish brooding wastefully,
Heaping the sullen forces baulked by life,
Harvesting blackness, gathering up rage,
Till at the last the spark, the seed of fire
Leaps from the cloud, and after comes the roar,
The deluge and the dire destructiveness,
And fields of tender thought are laid in mire?

But is there not the tempest-following calm,
The glitter, and the charm of a chilled air,
Songs poured while draggled plumes are fanned to dry,
And many buds' dun mantles beaten off,
While beauty new and naked opens and shines,
For every broken flower a score of heirs?
Does not the earth drink freshness audibly,
And all surviving things wax great and blow,

60

And with his strength renewed, the following sun
Make haste to wither the fallen out of sight,
And since they are dead to hurry them to dust?

Truly there is a tempest-following calm;
But if there be one of the mind I know not,
For I have never seen it. Her day is dim;
Her fairest day is one without alarms;
Cold was her dawn, colder shall be her night.
Her isle is circled by the hopeless sea
Which she may pass only by way of death:
Tempest or leaden calm, the grim north light
Is on her countenance reflected up,
And utterly bereaved of the soul's sun,
If such there be, sullen she labours on,
Still hoping faintly to be staunch enough
To weather the remaining tale of storms,
To make her landfall in the unknown place
Where the miraculous freshness falls like dew,
Where the song leaps while draggled plumage dries,
And on her face the sun incredible,
Long-fabled, legendary, and unhoped-for, shines.

CALL NOT TO ME

Call not to me when summer shines,
Death, for in summer I will not go;
When the tall grass falls in whispering lines
Call not loud from the shades below;
While under the willow the waters flow,
While willow waxes and waters wane,
When wind is slumbrous and water slow,
And woodbine waves in the wandering lane,
Call me not, for you call in vain,   .
Vain in the time when flowers blow.

61

But I will hear you when all is bare;
Call and welcome when leaves lie low;
When the dry bents hiss in the raving air
And shepherds from eastward smell the snow;
When the mead is left for the wind to mow,
And the storm is woodman to all the sere,
When hail is the seed the heavens sow,
When all is deadly and naught is dear –
Call and welcome, for I shall hear,
I shall be ready to rise and go.

TO THE SOUL

that she would cease from troubling

Feared and adored, the guest unsatisfied,
Chaos-derived and destined to the abyss,
The keystone of all mysteries,
Scourge of the flesh and urgent guide,
Why troublest thou me?
Holding out crowns and stars, great wounds and flames,
And whispering in the affrighted ear
Intolerable duties heaped with fear,
Dread laws, unutterable names –
What have I to do with thee?
Is life so light it should be burdened so,
Labour so sweet, death fair,
That thou with thorny doubts the way dost strow,
With portents fillest the air?
When I rejoice thou mournest low,
And in my dreaming thou art there.

How kind the ancient legends sound,
Of soulless Nymphs, that dwell
Within the rough bark's narrow round,
Or in pure springs; and those that tell

Of the small race, the unseen kind,
Strange in a perfect happiness,
That in the moonlight dress
Their round, and darting with the wind
Westward still leave the dawn behind?
Free of thy chains they sing,
And unafraid may prance in many a ring.

And beasts that are so still,
Soft eye, silk flank, sleek brow,
Sweet breath beneath the wide horns' bow,
Calm as their own calm hill,
Pensively grazing on a row,
Or by the wandering water laid
Beneath the oak's all but immortal shade —
Thou offerest them no star of tears,
No crown of blood,
No voice of heart-arresting fears,
No life that must be understood!

Flowers and trees, beauty and majesty,
Are perfect from the seed;
After no heaven I hear them sigh,
Not for the soul's sake have they need
To watch and weep, to groan and bleed:
The great boughs rise and fall
Like a contented breast, and that is all;
The blossom's countenance
Looketh on high with argent glance,
Then sheds her life in radiance.

Soul, though I may not cease
Under thy rod to groan, yet pause awhile;
Let me beguile
Some moments with a kind of peace;
Where for a little space
The way is green and level, O have grace!
Let me here stay, fetch sobbing breath,
Forbear the thought of death,

Sit trembling down, and wipe away
The sweat that falls upon the clay:
And O if there be water by
Let me draw near
To drown this fever in the mirrored sky,
To bless my ear
With liquid echoes, murmurs dear;
Still, still to hear the lonely Muse
Let fall her voice amid the dews,
And be possessed
But for a moment, by her rest!

REFLECTION

The winter falls and the winds groan;
God shall remain though I be gone.
I loved my life, I desired joy;
This was a fault, this was a toy.
An immortality I had
When I was young; then was I glad;
In summertime I felt no rue
For what the certain frost would do.
Ah bitter beauty, thou art delusion,
Though true enough I know to be
The horror and the dire confusion
That a clear vision shows to me.
Enough; give me my proven mail,
My arms of faith that cannot fail:
I cleave the chaos and prevail.

THE VIPER

Barefoot I went and made no sound;
The earth was hot beneath:
The air was quivering around,
The circling kestrel eyed the ground
And hung above the heath.

There in the pathway stretched along
The lovely serpent lay:
She reared not up the heath among,
She bowed her head, she sheathed her tongue,
And shining stole away.

Fair was the brave embroidered dress,
Fairer the gold eyes shone:
Loving her not, yet did I bless
The fallen angel's comeliness;
And gazed when she had gone.

HELP, GOOD SHEPHERD

Turn not aside, Shepherd, to see
How bright the constellations are,
Hanging in heaven, or on the tree;
The skyborn or terrestrial star

Brood not upon; the waters fleet,
Willows, or thy crown-destined thorn,
Full of her rubies, as is meet,
Or whitening in the eye of morn,

Pause not beside: shepherds' delight,
The pipe and tabor in the vale,
And mirthful watchfires of a night,
And herdsman's rest in wattled pale,

Forsake, though dearly earned: and still
Sound with thy crook the darkling flood,
Still range the sides of shelvy hill
And call about in underwood:

For on the hill are many strayed,
Some held in thickets plunge and cry,
And the deep waters make us afraid.
Come then and help us, or we die.

THANKSGIVING FOR A FAIR SUMMER

Now, before the wheat
Standing so nobly, falls:
Ere yet the first owl calls,
Or that thin sickle and fleet
Of harvest moon her earliest quarter passes,
Or the ground-frost may crisp the twice-mown grasses:
Now let me sing
My quiet stave, when redbreast too
Sings in, as I beneath, the yew:
Before they bring
The apples home, and once again
The equinox beats down the leaves in rain.

We had thought summer dead:
Year upon year
Prone in the furrow lay the smutted ear;
More wan than red
Hung tasteless fruit; flowers made earth their bier:
Kine to the lowering sky
Frowned in mute patience, and the hooded hind
Driving them home, in the soft ruts plodded by
With streaming shoulders and a heart unkind,
Sullen and bowed
Against a swagging heap of swollen cloud.

But now hot camomile in headlands grows,
Coarse-smelling as from toil of reaping; bees
Their delicate harvest in the rusty rows
Of scarlet bean, and woodbine that still blows,
Though flower with berry, gather and do not cease:
No mushroom yet, for dryness of the leas:
No leaf too early sere, for droughty root,
Drops from the trees,
But grave broad green guards the thick purple fruit.

Not only thanks for ample grain,
And apple that shall give her wine
As in old seasons, strong again;
Not for low streams where lilies shine
In many a pool unvexed by flood,
Unvexed by aught but boys at play:
Not only for the sun in the blood
And the long, blest, eventless day;

But chiefly for the sign,
For the fair time as token of grace
That life is yet benign,
That this our race
Still doth possess a pleasant place:
For many a doubt
Assails us, and might overthrow,
Were not the bow
Of blessing high in heaven hung out;
Our time is dark,
And save such miracle as this
Where is the mark
To steer by, in our bitter mysteries?

EARLY RISING

I arose early, O my true love!
I was awake and wide
To see the last star quenched above
And the moon lying on her side.

I saw the tops of the tall elms shine
Over the mist on the lea,
And the new bells upon the bine
Opened most silently;
And in the foggy dew the kine
Lay still as rocks in the sea.

The foggy dew lay on the flower
Silver and soft and chaste:
The turtle in her oaken tower
To waken made no haste:
Slept by her love another hour
And her two young embraced.

Mine was the solemn silence then,
And that clean tract of sky:
There was no smoke from hearths of men,
As yet no one went by:
The beast of night had sought his den,
The lark not climbed on high.

It was an hour of Eden; yea,
So still the time and slow,
I thought the sun mistook his way,
And was bewildered so
That coming he might bring a day
Lost since a thousand years ago:

A day of innocence and mirth,
A birds' day, day of prayer,
When every simple tongue on earth
A song or psalm might bear:

When love of God was something worth,
And holiness not killed with care.

But even while musing so, I laid
Flame to the gathered wood:
The sullying smoke swept up the glade,
Abashed the morning stood:
And in the mead the milking-maid
Called up the kine with accents rude.

And I was sad, O my true love,
For the love left unsaid:
I will sing it to the turtle-dove
That hugs her high-built bed:
I will say it to the solemn grove
And to the innocent dead.

OF SILENCE AND THE AIR

Here where the cold pure air is filled with darkness
graced but by Hesper and a comet streaming,
censed by the clean smoke from a herdsman's hearthstone
        I stand with silence:

void of desire, but full of contemplation
both of these herds and of the gods above them:
mindful of these, and offering submission
        to those immortal.

Older than they, the frosty air about me
speaks to the flocks like careful age, like winter,
saying, Seek shelter: to the gods, I know ye:
        and to me nothing

save but that silence is the truth: the silent
stars affirm nothing, and the lovely comet
silent impending, like a nymph translated
     abides in heaven.

Shall not I also stand and worship silence
till the cold enter, and the heart, the housewife,
spin no more, but sit down silent in the presence
     of the eternal?

BURIED TREASURE

Truth I sought, and truth I found,
Wandering enchanted ground

Where among the dusty rocks
Grows the twin-stemmed Paradox,

Throwing from the single root
Sable flower and golden fruit.

There I watched till I could tell
Where her midnight shadow fell,

And delved a diamond from the sand
Too heavy for my human hand.

Hold me not false that cannot bring
Nor show to you the magic thing:

Under the dual I divine
The one, but cannot make it mine.

THE OLD WOMAN

She reigns in the tarred cottage in the corn,
Clothed on with power, where her docile mate
Haunts rather than inhabits. To her state
Come suppliant both the dead and the unborn,
And village lovers of their loves forlorn;
And there sit down the aimless desolate.
These she delivers, these lays clean and straight,
These does she counsel, smiling without scorn:
And for these wretched, from her look severe
And winter-bright shines forth Philosophy,
A mind still satisfied with what must be,
Nobility of faith, and quiet breath.
They live, they sleep, take comfort, knowing her
Handmaid to love, priestess of life and death.

STORMCOCK IN ELDER

In my dark hermitage, aloof
From the world's sight and the world's sound,
By the small door where the old roof
Hangs but five feet above the ground,
I groped along the shelf for bread
But found celestial food instead:

For suddenly close at my ear,
Loud, loud and wild, with wintry glee,
The old unfailing chorister
Burst out in pride of poetry;
And through the broken roof I spied
Him by his singing glorified.

Scarcely an arm's-length from the eye,
Myself unseen, I saw him there;
The throbbing throat that made the cry,
The breast dewed from the misty air,
The polished bill that opened wide
And showed the pointed tongue inside:

The large eye, ringed with many a ray
Of minion feathers, finely laid,
The feet that grasped the elder-spray:
How strongly used, how subtly made
The scale, the sinew, and the claw,
Plain through the broken roof I saw;

The flight-feathers in tail and wing,
The shorter coverts, and the white
Merged into russet, marrying
The bright breast to the pinions bright,
Gold sequins, spots of chestnut, shower
Of silver, like a brindled flower.

Soldier of fortune, northwest Jack,
Old hard-times' braggart, there you blow!
But tell me ere your bagpipes crack
How you can make so brave a show,
Full-fed in February, and dressed
Like a rich merchant at a feast.

One-half the world, or so they say,
Knows not how half the world may live;
So sing your song and go your way,
And still in February contrive
As bright as Gabriel to smile
On elder-spray by broken tile.

THE LOST HERMITAGE

Templo valedixi cum osculo... SAMUEL JOHNSON

I'll none of Time:
I leave this place? this roof come down?
This is a graveyard jest, a dream
Too hard for rhyme:
We'll laugh at it when we sit down
Before God's Christmas fire, and tell
Our tales of worms, and ghosts, and hell,
That our eternal hearth securer seem.

My heart dwells here,
In rotten hut on weeping clay;
Tends here her useful herbs, her bloom;
Will not away,
May not be startled to one tear,
Is tenant of her little room
For ever, though they rase
Her cell, and rear a prison in its place.

Stockdove in oak,
Stormcock in elder, finch in thorn,
The blackbird in the quicken, jay,
Starling that spoke
Under the roof before the day,
Titmouse abhorred when damsons bud
And song-thrush hatched in cup of mud:

Frost on the grass,
The lonely morning, the still kine,
Grief for the quick, love for the dead;
The little hill's unchanging line
And nightingale so near my bed,
Pass and return, return and pass,
This time like many a time that was,
Many to be,
Swelling and lapsing seasons lulling me:

All these are laid
Safe up in me, and I will keep
My dwelling thus though it be gone:
My store is not in gold, but made
Of toil and sleep
And wonder walking all alone;
So time's brought low,
My heart's above all he can bring,
And forth in spite of him will go
To gather acorns: ay and sing.

AS WHEN THE FAITHFUL

As when the faithful return to valleys beloved,
little lamenting the winter, alone with the pensive
genius, the soul of the place, and when the profane ones
fly with the summer, and lewdness and folly are vanished:
so I with thine image at last shall abide in silence,
as one who has well kept the outposts against the enemy,
even the Cyprian: when those who lightly possess thee,
now, shall deride, shall forget, or haply shall hate thee,
mine shalt thou be in dateless eternal affection.
Quiet and clean is the house, and here I await thee:
thou by familiar groves, by the river of water,
under the snow-laden yew, the sun-gilded rose,
reverend with years, with youth immortally blooming,
silent advancest, and sittest down in my dwelling.

O WHERE IS THE DWELLING

O where is the dwelling I love the most,
And what but the one poor place can please,
Where the penny I lost and the faith I lost
Lie buried beneath enchanted trees?

O there is the dwelling I love the most,
And thither for ever my feet are bound,
Where the youth I lost and the love I lost
Lie buried, lie buried in holy ground!

SOUL'S EASTER

Fast and far out in time she is gone,
To see with her own eyes
The ruddy sun and the white moon
Out of the grave arise:

And still to the one point she moves,
However hardly or far,
To see her love and all her loves
Raised up above the morning star.

WEEPING WATER, LEAPING FIRE

Weeping water, leaping fire,
God and my grave are my desire.
With swarming strife and scanty joy,
Little ease and long annoy,
I am damned and drowned in rue –
With love then what have I to do?

With chaste stillness, blessed peace,
No annoy and utter ease,
Lulled in morning's lap I lie
And mend my sorrows in the sky.
I am redeemed and flown above –
Then what have I to do with love?

Heaven is stillness, motion hell,
When I stir not I am well.
Wake me not, for I would be
Laid where quiet waits on me.
Lovely boy, I know you lie:
Frown as you will, but pass me by.

SATURN'S COUNSEL

O lullaby both lead and gold,
Care no more, too careful head:
How they lied to thee who told
That the gold outweighs the lead!
Take no taper, darkling creep
To where beauty lies asleep
And old love and kindness keep:
As to a celestial bride
Steal in, lie down by honour's side;
Make that place your citadel
Where all virtue comes to dwell;
Since your fate to satisfy
Gold in lead must quiet lie.

APOLOGY

Have I, you ask, my fate forgot,
This veering mind, this flying breath,
Presumptuously, whose song is not
Ravished by love nor tamed by death?

O no: so deeply have I read
In love and death, I have descried
That Presence where even death lies dead,
And even the Cyprian veils her pride.

SUDDEN HEAVEN

All was as it had ever been –
The worn familiar book,
The oak beyond the hawthorn seen,
The misty woodland's look:

The starling perched upon the tree
With his long tress of straw –
When suddenly heaven blazed on me,
And suddenly I saw:

Saw all as it would ever be,
In bliss too great to tell;
For ever safe, for ever free,
All bright with miracle:

Saw as in heaven the thorn arrayed,
The tree beside the door;
And I must die – but O my shade
Shall dwell there evermore.

THE BUBBLE

Thus with the world: the virgin sphere
First but in candid white arrayed,
Ageing, must suffer to appear
The coloured continents, which fade

Rose into green and thinner blue,
Then sickly bronze, the dying thought;
Then deathly spots of blackish hue –
So breaks, and vanishes to nought.

Woe's me, born to the blackish death,
To the doomed bubble's final pain!
Yet it was blown of living breath,
Which the large air receives again.

THE PARADOX

Our death implicit in our birth,
We cease, or cannot be;
And know when we are laid in earth
We perish utterly.

And equally the spirit knows
The indomitable sense
Of immortality, which goes
Against all evidence.

See faith alone, whose hand unlocks
All mystery at a touch,
Embrace the awful Paradox
Nor wonder overmuch.

URANIA

Winter and night, the white frost and the darkness
fall, and the hands of life release the spirit;
gladly she goes hence to her starry pasture.

Frostbound, the plough leans idle on the headland;
now the benighted hind forsakes the furrow;
earth is at peace, no longer vexed with labour.

With still delight the soul receives the omen,
thinks on her travail in the sowing season,
calmly remembers all the heat of harvest:

knows that the end is fairest; sees the heavens
hung with creation: in the woody valley
sees on the earth one star that steals toward her.

It is Urania: through the darkened woodland
now she advances: now she brings her vestal
lamp to the tomb, with nameless consolation.

THE UNICORN

Hate me or love, I care not, as I pass
To those hid citadels
Where in the depth of my enchanted glass
The changeless image dwells;
To where for ever blooms the nameless tree;
For ever, alone and fair,
The lovely Unicorn beside the sea
Is laid, and slumbers there.

Give or withhold, all's nothing, as I go
On to those glimmering grounds
Where falling secretly and quiet as snow
The silent music sounds;
Where earth is withered away before the eyes,
And heaven hangs in the air,
For in the oak the bird of paradise
Alights, and triumphs there.

Slay me or spare, it matters not: I fly
Ever, for ever rest
Alone and with a host: in the void sky
There do I build my nest:
I lay my beams from star to star, and make
My house where all is bare;
Hate, slay, withhold, I rear it for thy sake
And thou art with me there.

FAIR IS THE WATER

Fair is the water when the land is fainting,
fair on the braided tresses of the barley:
fair as it falls from heaven to the rose, and
        lies in its bosom:

fair is the water when the wind is urging   ·
waves against land as horse against a city:
the wave-form at the crest of motion peerless,
        fair in its falling.

Fairest is water when the heart at evening
leads the fond feet to the familiar places:
fairest is water when it falls in silent
        dew where thou liest.

ON A CERTAIN PHILOSOPHY

Out of the order, the calm, the mighty conclusions
Breathe as of balm, sing triumph, like adamant shine.
Lions lie there amid lily and violet sleeping:
Fire arises, and delicate dew descends to assuage it.
Sphere within sphere cries thunderously Hosanna,
Space beyond space extends virginal, holy and silent;
The sacred desert of silence, the sacred oasis of sound.
There is no stain, stainless thou mayest believe this:
This is the bridegroom, and this the soul's marriage of honour.
Therefore consent.
           The spirit within her chamber,
Her lonely and maiden tower, leans at the lattice,
Contemplates, ravished with love, the ascending glory:
Her heart leaps out to the horsemen, leaps to the warriors,
Delights in the spears, joins itself to the wonder:
But her feet know not why they should move to descend,
And her hand is still, is still on the latch of the window;
She will not go down, and never will she surrender.
It is but a matter of raiment, as ever with women.
She will not go down clothed in the weeds of her nonage;
She has worn space and time too long, she is weary
Of beautiful space, of intricate many-hued time:
Scanty and tarnished they seem: she waits for the bridal
Robe of eternity, the only garment of honour.

CAGED LION

You are afraid. You do not dare
Up to the Lion to lift your eyes,
And unashamed his beauty share
As once in that lost Paradise.

81

With fallen cunning lay the snare,
With fearful glee shoot home the bar;
Show him for pence imprisoned there –
In a foul sepulchre a star.

His maned neck of massy girth
Only one Arm in love enfolds:
His beauty humbled to the earth
Only my wrathful God beholds.

THE THREE POPLARS

I am ashamed: three spirits standing tall
On the low ridge, and only heaven,
Morning in heaven beyond, I promised you.
You've come so far with me too; ah, what shame
These three torn hulks cower under: poor aliens,
Short-lived, soft-wooded, in this windvexed place
They perished: here the brushwood-stealing boys,
The large white beetle-worm, the wind, long rains,
And last year's drought prodigious, prevailed.
Are you still patient? be kind, return,
Come help me search for them lost by the way:
They are worth much. There, such short time ago,
They stand, the nymphs, the slender sisters dear,
Newflung to May the balsam of their hair:
Noble and young, adequate, love's trinity.
Hang we our harps upon them: for the pipe,
Muse, then play up with "pastourelle gentille."
Did you hear Honour's trumpet blow? alas,
Silence must answer, and among these virgins
I wish not for the lyre of love. Go play,
Go celebrate them sweetly where they soar
From the low ridge, and only heaven,
Only lost heaven looks through their tender gold.

82

THE STRAWBERRY PLANT

Above the water, in her rocky niche,
She sat enthroned and perfect; for her crown
One bud like pearl, and then two fairy roses
Blanched and yet ardent in their glowing hearts:
One greenish berry spangling into yellow
Where the light touched the seed: one fruit achieved
And ripe, an odorous vermilion ball
Tight with completion, lovingly enclasped
By the close cup whose green chimed with the red,
And showered with drops of gold like Danaë:
Three lovely sister leaves as like as peas,
Young but full-fledged, dark, with a little down:
Two leaves that to a matron hue inclined;
And one the matriarch, that dressed in gold
And flushed with wine, thought her last days her best.
And here and there a diamond of dew
Beamed coolly from the white, smiled from the gold,
Silvered the down, struck lightning from the red.
The overhanging rock forbade the sun,
Yet she was all alight with water-gleams
Reflected, like the footlights at a play:
Perfection's self, and (rightly) out of reach.

THE APPLE-TREE

From the old woodland, whence I bring
Too much decay, too little spring,
I come, and in a southward place
Where March first sees the primrose' face,
I with a sharp delight behold
A shaft of light, a tower of gold:
A dear and blessed thing to see,
The lovely laden Apple-tree.
I sit me down his boughs below,

The cold and tortuous musings go:
I from the lowest branches take
Four apples for my childhood's sake;
One that I may remember still
The loved, the lovely daffodil,
And never find that deepest gloom
That has forgot the apple-bloom:
One for high summer, when in light
The vast elms quiver in my sight,
And when the small green apples hide
In the thick green on every side:
When in the oozy water-nooks
The muffling cresses hush the brooks;
One for dear harvest, labour's crown,
When hard hands lay the sickle down,
And this hale tree his kindly fruit
Drops all about the mossy root:
And one for when the chilly rain
Must sweep the ploughland and the plain,
Unfeared, unhated, when by thee,
My lovely living Apple-tree,
I lean in shelter from the shower
And count the buds, and dream the flower:
And winter is no more to fear
Than it were Granfer drawing near;
Than pleasant Granfer, plodding on
By fallows whence the wheat is gone,
By finchy copses, whence among
The sense of God exhales in song,
To where in the warm stackyard still
The Harvest shines upon the hill.

MY GOD BEHOLDS ME

(Hymns to the Noumenon)

1.   *The lion-seraph*
To love the Lion I will dare;
He waves in heaven his flames of hair:
Comet of beauty, through each limb
The entire being informeth him:
He could crush my every bone,
Yet this is but phenomenon.
My secret spirit sees him all,
Through the rent veil, the crumbling wall.
In joy this great archangel old
My glorious God, and I, behold.

2.   *Two sparrows for a farthing*
Strange pang of conscience for the weed, whose beauty
none celebrates, and for the stone imprisoned
in one poor form, deprived of growth and movement,
          loveless, unhonoured!

Live they indeed, or are they but illusion,
the stone, the weed, and the destroying insect:
what is their portion and their just appraisement?
          For we reject them.

Desolate they stand in deserts of illusion;
from the dark stone I hear the voice of weeping:
they stream with light in heaven, where for ever
          their God beholds them.

3.   *The Spanish painting*
Static, weighed down with riches, sad with pomp,
The watching shadows menace the one gleam:
Dragon-like, brocade threatens the youthful hair;
Hands but express a sumptuous idleness,

All's done to serve the ceremonial.
Yet (star within a tomb) the painter here
Bursts the strong sepulchre, and to a sound
Terrible, of all chords in heaven and earth
From the black diapason to shrill white,
Bids the dead lord in majesty arise,
Makes fly the pentecostal dove, which soars
Out of the canvas, and strikes dead in the heart
The fell phenomenon, burns it away,
Leaving NOUMENON pulsing above time:
Which triumph my eternal God beholds.

   4.   *And thereon was ywritten a crowned A*
Some there be who rend and steal
Shreds from the real to patch the unreal;
To mend their hovel on the sands
Destroy the house not made with hands.
Fearing to lose what seems to flee,
They rob their own eternity.
But at the last all will not do,
The insulted fragments vanish too;
And mad in space and time they run,
Houseless in heaven, on earth undone.
My mind is fixed. If still unfound
My fair hewn stone, my plot of ground,
To build the house of love in space
Like that in its eternal place:
Why then on earth a houseless wretch,
No mud nor wattles will I fetch,
Far less from the sweet Mansion pull
Fair cornice or bright pinnacle
To botch a shapeless hovel, where
I should come to mere despair:
But wither in clean wind and rain
Till summoned I return again,
And enter, from the naked field,
That blissful place by God beheld.

5. *Not one is lost*
I see mankind, how it is vile;
        A cruel pain!
Sweet innocence, return awhile,
        I'll look again.
Lost innocence its candid eye
        Opes from the east,
From where it lay, where it doth lie,
        On my God's breast.

Damned by that look, dissolves the dream:
        O how I err!
In thy regard how bright they seem,
        Dear Lucifer
(Unfallen yet); how each one shows
        Worthy of love;
How each toward the end his spirit knows
        Doth calmly move!

The cloud closes, the candid eye
        Is dimmed, is gone,
But by the gleam left in the sky
        I'll wander on
Till Lucifer be Hesper in the west,
        And wrapped in gold
I the world's innocence upon the breast
        Of God behold.

THE BRIDGE

Where is the truth that will inform my sorrow?
I am sure myself that sorrow is not the truth.
These lovely shapes of sorrow are empty vessels
Waiting for wine: they wait to be informed.
Men make the vessels on either side of the river;
On this the hither side the artists make them,

And there over the water the workmen make them:
These frail, with a peacock glaze, and the others heavy,
Simple as doom, made to endure the furnace.
War shatters the peacock-jars: let us go over.

Indeed we have no choice but to go over.

There is always a way for those who must go over:
Always a bridge from the known to the unknown.
When from the known the mind revolts and despairs
There lies the way, and there we must go over.

O truth, is it death there over the river,
Or is it life, new life in a land of summer?
The mind is an empty vessel, a shape of sorrow,
Fill it with life or death, for it is hollow,
Dark wine or bright, fill it, let us go over.

Let me go find my truth, over the river.

THE BEAUTIFUL NEGRESS

Her gait detached her from the moving throng:
Like night, advancing with long pace and slow,
Or like unhurrying fate she seemed to go,
By an eternal Purpose borne along.
An unregretful elegiac Song
Swelled in her wake; she gathered up my woe
Into epitome, and left it so;
Still dark, but made harmonious and strong.
O solemn Beauty, when upon my way
You walked in majesty, did not the tear
Leap up to crown you with more light than day?
Did not the silent voice within the ear
Cry Fly with her to the soul's Africa,
Night, tragedy, the veiled, the end prefer?

A SOLEMN MEDITATION

These discords and these warring tongues are gales
Of the great autumn: how shall winter be?
Of love, of summer speak not; rather pray
That in the warmer vales
Some may survive: that some winged seeds may flee
Into the mountains far away,
That such may see
Their spring, and spread their green in unimagined day.

Think not that I complain, that I must go
Under the ground, unblossomed, unfulfilled;
Though our stem freeze, in the earth's bosom I
And you sleep: under snow
We shall be saved, though winter blow so wild
That not a tree remain under the sky:
This hydra life will not take no,
More withering now, more blossoming by and by.

It goes down to the nadir: never fear,
Down to the dark, go down, as deep as hell:
The swift fall wings the ascent: close eyes
And hurl head down and sheer
Into the black of life unfathomable;
Down to the nethermost dive: the prize
Only to him who the night-hemisphere
Can girdle like the sun: gone! it is well.

Naked upon the bosom of my God,
Bereft of all save the Unmanifest,
My blossom nipped and my leaf shorn,
In the great bitter dark I touch his breast:
Praise him that I was born,
Cast in the utter gulf those rags and weeds,
My ruined hopes, my summer's short delight,
And my abortive deeds,
Even as children leave their toys at night.

Perusing death with these shade-coloured eyes,
I have surprised the secret of the strong,
Drunk of the nether springs of fearlessness;
Stolen the knowledge of the wise:
Seen where the great rocks and glooms among
The rubied treasure burns in its recess;
Fallen, have fought and thrust
My way to where the immortal lies enwombed in dust.

Then Alleluia all my gashes cry;
My woe springs up and flourishes from the tomb
In her lord's likeness terrible and fair;
Knowing her root, her blossom in the sky
She rears: now flocking to her branches come
The paradisal birds of upper air,
Which Alleluia cry, and cry again,
And death from out the grave replies Amen.

THE TASK

Reverse the flight of Lucifer,
Hurl back to heaven the fallen star;
Recall Eve's fate, establish her
Again where the first glories are:
Again where Eden's rivers are.

Thrust back contention, merge in one
Warring dualities, make free
Night of the moon, day of the sun;
End the old war of land and sea,
Saying, There shall be no more sea.

With love of love now make an end;
Let male and female strive no more;
Let good and bad their quarrel mend
And with an equal voice adore;
The lion with the lamb adore.

Bow lofty saint, rise humble sin,
Fall from your throne, creep from your den:
The king, the kingdom is within,
That is for evermore, amen:
Was dead and is alive. Amen.

THE BAD GIRL

I saw her in her woodland place
When she was young, when we were young:
And there was fairness in her face
And a sweet verse upon her tongue.

The last red light made glancing ore
The mosses on the knotty tree:
The level rays in the covert's core
Made all the leafage fantasy;

Made the brown gold, and made her seem
(Who was, God knows, but common clay)
A noble thing, a lovely theme,
One that could not be cast away.

I cast away, I cast away
Things childish, and am not forlorn:
But she had better have died, the day
She stood so fair beneath the thorn.

Younger than I yet is she old;
None finds her honest, none finds her sweet:
Long past her beauty, she will scold,
Will beg and cozen, lie and cheat.

I as the woody medlar grow
And shall be ripe when I am rotten:
But like June's strawberry, even so
She, much enjoyed, is soon forgotten.

Yet like Ben Jonson's lily, she
Lent to her day a darling grace,
Remembered till unwept shall be
Laid in the loam her lilied face.

So, Saturn, upon Venus think,
And light esteem your armour tough:
Say, though the festering lily stink,
Strength without beauty's not enough.

JOY AND GRIEF

What of my Joy?
See how she fades;
While Grief, great growing boy,
Devours, invades;
He my whole having eats,
She finds no food,
And by my chimney sits
In dying attitude.

When she is gone
With Grief I'll dwell;
When we are left alone,
He, who can tell?
May gentler grow, and be
In my cold age
A comforter to me,
The wounds he gave, assuage.

Meanwhile I nourish both,
The devourer and the dying:
I am strong, I cast away sloth
And do but little sighing;

See the sad purity
Of the white sky and the stream!
On these, and the winter tree,
I will gaze, I will dream.

CLOSE, MORTAL EYES

Close, mortal eyes: open, my eyes in heaven.
On consolations that the poor devise,
On the clay image and the candles seven
          Close, mortal eyes.

Open upon the plains of the merry land,
Eternal eyes, on joy for ever whole:
Return with tidings I shall understand,
          Eyes of my soul.

The soul has eyes: alas, she has no tongue,
She has no word of all the mysteries,
No syllable that may be said or sung.
          Close, mortal eyes.

THE RETURN

So, since the battle goes so ill,
Let me lie down and dream of home:
To-night I'll lie upon the hill
Between the leaves and the loam:
Lie there where quiet was
Between the bough and the grass.

I know what tree the nightingale
Alights on when she sits to sing:
I know where the mist lies, with pale
Enchantment silvering
The long bed of the brook:
I know the meadows' look.

My long-uprooted lily smells,
And by lost forest-verges too
First woodbine, last hyacinth-bells
Breathe balm in the cold dew:
Breathe love to the cold heart
That could arise and depart;

To no end but to be old and poor,
To lose the good, and to get the bane:
To find no door like the rotting door
Which I find not again:
To weep in my bed at night
And forget the tear of delight.

THOUGHT AGAINST DROUGHT

O fair befall what flourished so fair,
All in the wet green wood!
The vale-lily in shadow there
Like a clean spirit stood:

Solomon's seal under broad leaves
Hung down the serried flower,
And periwinkle under eaves
Nodded to feel the shower:

And though from the dank cottage wall
The grinning mildew glared,
What in the dry world might befall
I neither knew not cared.

94

TO J.S. COLLIS

Live unlamenting though obscure remaining:
be as the bird that in the desolate places
feeds her two young, and man-unheard is heard still
    to her God crying.

Die unaccursed though the universal
curse be abroad: for of her God remembered
·though the world burn, the spirit as a bird shall
    flee to her mountain.

ELEGY TO MARY

Mary, daughter of John White, woodman, of this parish,
           and of Susan his wife.
                She died
             June 25, 1821,
        in the XXth year of her age.

God's peace is the treasure of dead fools, Mary:
Here by thy stone I betray myself and secede
My fortified cities, here relapse, to the obsolete
Tending in weariness under thy white moss-rose:
Here become pensive, inviting cheap critics' derision.

Thee blank docility, negative chastity sufficed, Mary:
Gentle and good, remembered still for beauty;
Foolishly fading, and pearly in petty decline;
Nothing, if sweetness is naught, obedience vapid;
Nothing: then why through the valley remembered?

Safe lie the slender bones under the rose and the yew:
Secure is the tender spirit, unforgotten by simple
Minds that consider the grass; green is the weed,
The same that grew on the graves in thy time, Mary:
The thought of thee, like the form of the flower, unchanging.

95

Thee I behold as once I beheld the linnet
Lying with hard-wrung claw on the tender turf,
Dead, not dinting the beautiful mosses,
Green feather caressing dun feather, the petal of cranesbill
Minute and rosy, fallen upon its bosom.

I was a child, then my tear did not shame me;
Fittingly then might the bright lip quiver,
The undimmed eye overflow, the unfaded hair
Be drooped on the dead, and the little heart mourn,
Mourn in the minor mode for a little matter.

Grace is fled from the tear; now when I mourn,
Ashamed and in secret, seated amid corruption,
In the expanding universe hope too recedes,
Or in the diminishing sinks to a dying ember,
Drops through the boughs of time and eludes me for ever.

Yet there are days when mourning is done with, Mary;
Strange is my sorrow to thee: how far stranger my joy!
Far into space I see; in ocean of ether,
What is it swims there, in infinite orbit:
Who then are those, in glittering spiral ascending?

Even the eagles of God, the translated spirits,
A time, and times, and a time gone by and transcended;
All paradox seized and resolved, all evil consumed,
All fear soared above, the depth and the height reconciled,
The ultimate claimed, the great cry of unity uttered.

Then I behold the filthy orts and the carcases,
The gobbets, the offal of slaughter about me:
Then I behold myself, both savage and feeble,
Covered with creeping despairs: then dare I to glory,
Then stretch out the growing wing, and scream from the eyrie!

God's triumph is the treasure of the soul, Mary.

FELLOW-CREATURES

Unpublished poem, written 1938

The heart shall not be satisfied
Till all creatures hear its word:
The lion's love must be its pride,
Its joy the friendship of a bird.

It would be welcome in the lairs
Of lynxes, and lie down with them,
Would lean upon the sides of bears,
Stroke the wild peacock's diadem:

Confer with singing seals in caves,
With the tall ostrich in the sand,
And where the long liana waves
Touch the great ape's accomplished hand.

How shall the heart such rapture reach
Till the stiff tongue its manners mend,
To say to men, in human speech,
Beloved, immortal spirit, friend?

THE SOLITARY

You can do all without her aid,
Mother, round wife, and springing daughter,
And Maggie too, the moon-eyed maid,
So let her wander by the water:
Give her no task but to bring
The flowers for your Easter table;
Let her go out and see the spring
Returns again, let the birds' babble
Wake in her mind some vague access
Of comfort to her heaviness.

What will she fetch, what will she gather
From the soft lanes and hedgerows wet?
By the cool wood in the fresh weather
She seeks the wild white violet:
But what old pain, what lingering lack,
Makes her pull down the solemn leaf,
With knots of ivy-berries black
She should forget with winter's grief?
How can she with these virgins clear
Mingle the gloom of yester-year?

She leaves the silver willow waving,
The primrose by the gleaming ditches;
The cowslip is not worth her having,
Nor the great kingcup's harmless riches:
The sharp-starred celandine she passes,
She leaves aside that old delight,
The rosy daisy in the grasses:
And still intent on black and white
With violet and ivy she
Sets forth the unspoken tragedy.

AN OLD-FASHIONED SONG

Lay the hand on the breast,
Though that cannot still the heart:
The loveliest and the best
Is removed far apart:
Never in your wandering
Shall you find the holy thing.

Drop the eyelid on the eye,
Though that cannot stay the tear:
Be silent, unlamenting lie,
Though it may be many a year,
Many a long year before
One and one make two no more.

THE DOWNWARD-POINTING MUSE

True to the daemon, sorrowful and strong,
No fatal error yet, no ache to whisper
The nearest way to earth; dig the day long,
But pause at evening: see where Hesper
Clears the dark tree, and lights amid the dews
The downward-pointing Muse.

She knows the star, and she regards it not,
Pavilioned in the citron-coloured eve:
She knows the plant clustering her hallowed spot,
Loves dearly, but doth leave
Both bud and star, and answers with no word
The day's last darling bird.

Fair spirit, turn, rewarding with a tear,
If smiles are not to be,
The light from heaven, the flower clear,
The high and haunted tree:
Return for rays, for odours, for the choice
Last song some look, some voice!

She will not be invoked: so be content
Thus purely to be motioned to the shade;
She means no anger, no lament,
But mirrors heaven, where she was made:
With august look, with neither smile nor frown
She stands there, pointing down:

Down to the fixed and universal grave,
To the deep mines, the dreadful core;
To the dark Mother, to the funereal wave
Of buried rivers over nameless ore,
To secret vaults, the wombs of primal fear,
And all the demons there!

Let it be so, if she, the nightingale,
The single star, the clear nocturnal bloom,
The fair delicious lily of the vale,
Stands glimmering through the gloom:
Let it be so, and hers the lamp shall be
To light the mystery.

Faithful as death, she answers in a dream:
Behold, she says, an earth as clear as glass,
Whose dreadful heart, burning like cherubim,
My still more fervid gaze doth pass:
And downward still, my heavenly one
Points to the buried Sun.

THE VINE IN BLOOM

It matters not to grow old, when the vine is breaking:
The years have no weight when the holy vine is in bloom:
Soon I must be sleeping, but this shall still be waking,
The promise of birth is breathed in the word of doom;
She gives me the flower now, then the cluster that comes in its room,
But soon I must be giving and the vine taking.

There is no grudge, dear root; there is no quarrel.
Deep in your debt, I leave you the last word.
I look from between your leaves and behold the sorrel
Mare in the field with her foal: and the speckled bird,
Murmuring her care and her busy kindness, is heard
Nourishing next year's songs in the bonny laurel.

TIME'S FOOL

Time's fool, but not heaven's: yet hope not for any return.
The rabbit-eaten dry branch and the halfpenny candle
Are lost with the other treasure: the sooty kettle
Thrown away, become redbreast's home in the hedge, where the
    nettle
Shoots up, and bad bindweed wreathes rust-fretted handle.
Under that broken thing no more shall the dry branch burn.

Poor comfort all comfort: once what the mouse had spared
Was enough, was delight, there where the heart was at home;
The hard cankered apple holed by the wasp and the bird,
The damp bed, with the beetle's tap in the headboard heard,
The dim bit of mirror, three inches of comb:
Dear enough, when with youth and with fancy shared.

I knew that the roots were creeping under the floor,
That the toad was safe in his hole, the poor cat by the fire,
The starling snug in the roof, each slept in his place:
The lily in splendour, the vine in her grace,
The fox in the forest, all had their desire,
As then I had mine, in the place that was happy and poor.

BURNING THE BEE-TREE

Lay on the fire their ancient hold,
Which they left when the tree died:
We threw their tower down on the mould,
And split it open wide,
But they had taken away their gold,
And there was none inside.

Nothing but the embalming stain,
And a few shards of comb,
And a breath as of the clover-plain
Still lingered in their home,
With skeletons of robbers slain,
Who had too rich a tomb.

Up sweetly on the autumn air
Spiced funeral vapours rise:
What do you see above, what fair
Visions salute your eyes,
What reverend memories repair
The breach of centuries?

I smell the death of song, I hear
That fair bird's last lament;
I see the shades of heroes near,
About their purple tent;
I see the rich, the dabbled hair,
The damasked armour rent.

And pure, on humble air, the song
Of love is heard to chime,
The oak's unchanging leaves among
In an unchanging rhyme,
For the bees remain the same so long
They keep no count of time.

The labour, and the bitter sting,
The cells' meticulous range,
Honey, which makes a perishing thing
Immortal, do not change;
Life, make one couplet that I sing
As deathless, and as strange!

AN OLD WOMAN SPEAKS OF THE MOON

She was urgent to speak of the moon: she offered delight
And wondering praise to be shared by the girl in the shop,
Lauding the goddess who blessed her each sleepless night
Greater and brighter till full: but the girl could not stop.

She turned and looked up in my face, and hastened to cry
How beautiful was the orb, how the constant glow
Comforted in the cold night the old waking eye:
How fortunate she, whose lodging was placed that so

She in the lonely night, in her lonely age,
She from her poor lean bed might behold the undying
Letter of loveliness written on heaven's page,
The sharp silver arrows leap down to where she was lying.

The dying spoke love to the immortal, the foul to the fair,
The withered to the still-flowering, the bound to the free:
The nipped worm to the silver swan that sails through the air:
And I took it as good, and a happy omen to me.

LOVE AND THE CHILD

Like mist in the holy morning, the thin veil of love
Mantles him over, and colours all he is conscious of;
Till time like the mounting sun rolling the mist to the crests
Bares all but the secret parts and the lips and the breasts.

Leave him the light shade, leave him his rosy tent;
Rend not the thin stuff, for death enters in at the rent:
Touch him but lightly, and see that you speak only truth,
For the sake of the secret parts and the breast and the mouth.

THE PRIMORDIAL CELL

Think, muse on her, do not forget our common mother.

She is to me as the old withered mother of many
Spinning beside the doorway of her crumbling cottage,
Dreaming of those long fled from her, those nobler faces,
And glorying darkly in her children's fairer children:
Too humble to look for gratitude; and O too sunken
In aged-infant dream to care that many suffer:
Poor beyond reach of pity, and in huge indifference
Wealthy, though all her progeny die in the world's ruin.

Glorious, and justified eternally, is our mother.

For if we perished all, she would arise a virgin,
Immaculate as on the third day of creation,
Capable of bearing new gods and greater heroes,
Conceiving a more ravishing rose, a lovelier lily.
Determined to outdo our vaunted glories, she,
Triumphing over our vacant places, would nobly fill them.

She eats disaster: war and famine are her plough-oxen.
Ruin this star, she would betake her to another.
Down dread eternities she looks, not for perfection.

She spins forgotten at the doorway of her cottage.
Think, muse on her, do not forget our common mother.

STRUGGLING WHEAT

(From the French of Jeanne Perdriel-Vaissière)

Struggling wheat, weighed down with rain,
Which the sun scarce dries again,
Under a treacherous cloud unkind,
Between two passions of the wind:

Scanty wheat that cannot veil
The doomed nest and young of the quail
From the hawk that in the sky
Planes with ruin in his eye:

Child of the cold grudging clay,
Weeping when not parched away,
By the inconstant season harried
Even till you are cut and carried:

Still you strive with effort grim
To touch the overhanging limb
Of the tree that keeps the sun
For himself, and leaves you none.

Blackened wheat, and wheat of tears,
Earth-besmirched and ruined ears,
Brave as an ill-fated man
Who does, though dying, what he can:

Take from this transient mind and eye
This look, this thought of sympathy;
Not leaden pity, but the love
Your gallant life is worthy of.

THE STOCKDOVE

Close in the hollow bank she lies,
Soiling with clay her azure dress:
Then slowly lifts that head, whose eyes
Have given a name to gentleness.
O is she caught, and is she snared,
Or why so still, and perched so low?
She is not ruffled, is not scared,
And yet I watch, and cannot go.

And dumbly comes the hard reply;
Death shakes her like a winter storm;
Then her round head she would put by,
As she was wont, in feathers warm:
Half lifts the wing, half turns the bill,
Then leans more lowly on the clay,
Sighs, and at last is quiet and still,
Sits there, and yet is fled away.

The epoch will not suffer me
To weep above such humble dead,
Or I could mourn a century
For all such woe unmerited:
For the soft eye, the feathers blue,
The voice more gentle than the rain,
The feet that dabbled in the dew,
We strew the field with poisoned grain.

My questioned spirit's sidelong look
From her old fortress answers me,
From where she reads her secret book
On the tall rock Infinity:
From where the innocent dead to that
High place is fled away from grief,
And whence as from an Ararat
She brings the silver olive-leaf.

IF YOU CAME

If you came to my secret glade,
      Weary with heat,
I would set you down in the shade,
      I would wash your feet.

If you came in the winter sad,
  Wanting for bread,
I would give you the last that I had,
  I would give you my bed.

But the place is hidden apart
  Like a nest by a brook,
And I will not show you my heart
  By a word, by a look.

The place is hidden apart
  Like the nest of a bird:
And I will not show you my heart
  By a look, by a word.

THE DIFFERENCE

There in the field hear the voice of the lark day-long
That leaps up loud with his love into the clear grey:
But if the nest were harried
And the mate that he married
Were fled from the place, he must cease from the song:
But you must sing ever in spite of all wrong,
Whatever is lost, strayed, or stolen away.

There by the water behold the beautiful face
Of the flower that looks up into the smile of the day:
But if the spring were failing,
Or the cold wind were wailing,
She would sink, would fall down there, would die in her grace:
But you must bloom still in the desolate place,
Whatever is frozen or withered away.

THE MILITARY HARPIST

Strangely assorted, the shape of song and the bloody man.

Under the harp's gilt shoulder and rainlike strings,
Prawn-eyed, with prawnlike bristle, well-waxed moustache,
With long tight cavalry legs, and the spurred boot
Ready upon the swell, the Old Sweat waits.

Now dies, and dies hard, the stupid, well-relished fortissimo,
Wood-wind alone inviting the liquid tone,
The voice of the holy and uncontending, the harp.

Ceasing to ruminate interracial fornications,
He raises his hands, and his wicked old mug is David's,
Pastoral, rapt, the king and the poet in innocence,
Singing Saul in himself asleep, and the ancient Devil
Clean out of countenance, as with an army of angels.

He is now where his bunion has no existence.
Breathing an atmosphere free of pipeclay and swearing,
He wears the starched nightshirt of the hereafter, his halo
Is plain manly brass with a permanent polish,
Requiring no oily rag and no Soldier's Friend.

His place is with the beloved poet of Israel,
With the wandering minnesinger and the loves of Provence,
With Blondel footsore and heartsore, the voice in the darkness
Crying like beauty bereaved beneath many a donjon,
O Richard! O king! where is the lion of England?
With Howell, Llewellyn, and far in the feral north
With the savage fame of the hero in glen and in ben,
At the morning discourse of saints in the island Eire,
And at nameless doings in the stone-circle, the dreadful grove.

Thus far into the dark do I delve for his likeness:
He harps at the Druid sacrifice, where the golden string
Sings to the golden knife and the victim's shriek.
Strangely assorted, the shape of song and the bloody man.

108

THE HUT

Whatever place is poor and small,
The Hut was poorer still,
Stuck, like a snail upon a wall,
On what we called a hill.

It leaned upon an apple-tree
Whose laden branches lay
On the hot roof voluptuously,
And murmured all the day.

One hand-broad window, full of boughs,
Mirrored the flaming hearth
As if the Dryad warmed her house
With fire from under earth;

And one the livid lasting-pea
And staring marigold,
The knotty oak and elder-tree
Showed in the morning cold.

The sapling ash had mined the floor,
The chimney flew the bine;
The doorway was without a door,
But flaunted eglantine.

The swallow built upon the beam,
The rat was much at home:
And there one foolish child would dream,
Where sorrow could not come.

A NATURAL SORROW

Silent as a falling leaf
To my heart there came a grief:
With a cold and pure despair,
Angerless, it settled there:
And must linger, and must stay,
Till it waste from mere decay,
Or till spring's uprushing tide
Thrust the skeleton aside.
I will not grudge to feel it so,
This dead leaf, this natural woe,
Neither will rage nor yet repine,
But let it lie there as a sign:
Simple as a pyramid
Where the royal dead are hid;
Naked as that ancient stone
Where *alas* is graved alone;
Humble as the tattered nest
Which once felt the thrush's breast,
And harmless as the bustling wren
That trips about it now and then.

THE TIGRESS

The raging and the ravenous,
The nocturnal terror in gold,
Red-fire-coated, green-fire-eyed,
The fanged, the clawed, the frightful leaper
Great-sinewed, silent walker,
Tyrant of all the timid, the implacable
Devil of slaughter, the she-demon
Matchless in fury, matchless love
Gives her whelps in the wildernesses.

Cleaning the stains of slaughter
From her jaws with tongue and forearm,
She licks her young and suckles them
Delicately as a doe:
She blood-gutted is the angel
To their blindness, she is minister
Between life and these feeble young
In barren places, where no help is.

Or man-imprisoned often disdaining
To rear her royal brood, though cheated
Into bearing, she abandons
All at birth, and bids them die.
Utter love and utter hatred
Cannot compromise; she gives
Her whole being to their being
Or rejects them into death.

No thought intervenes; her justice
Is not mind-perverted: O tigress,
Royal mother without pity,
Could but one thought arise within
That greatly-sculptured skull, behind
The phosphorus eyes compunction burn,
Well might it be for all these millions
Mind-infected, mother-betrayed:
No beast so hapless as a man.

RARE BIRDS

They tempt the bittern back to nest,
He beats the unwarlike drum
Where Danish bones with Saxon rest,
While through the night there come
Again long-exiled beauties to their former home.

111

But the bird Peace withholds her wing:
She cannot build and be
The fireless Phoenix of the spring
By our green northern sea,
Nor feed beside the Mediterranean tranquilly.

O fair in that remembered oak
She smoothed her silver snow,
And fed her sacred young, and spoke
Like beauty from the bough:
But no one knows where she inhabits now.

1938

O when will they let them love
As they are dying to do,
Men, creatures, brave spirits, friends,
The flower and the wonder of life?
They weep and die, and their bones
Mingle in earth, as never
In life could their aching minds,
Lost and parted, betrayed and forsaken!

They are shreds of a garment of gold
Flapping from many a thorn;
The sharp-edged fragments of a great vessel
That should be holding the wine;
The stones of a princely house,
Showing each some feature of grace,
But broken and scattered asunder,
The mortar being perished.

The greatest harvests of time –
Abundance, if fairly divided –
Are burned or thrown in the sea:

112

The mind, with its burden of love
Corrupting, now heavily weighs
The means of a myriad deaths.

The gentle are ground into earth
And the tender despised:
Honour's an ass-head, a bauble,
The mark of a profitless fool;
The good man's goal is the grave,
His secret longing extinction.

The numberless warring voices
There keep unanimous silence,
The minds that conceived the slaughter
Are merged in harmless oblivion,
The hand that snatched up the weapon
Lies still, forgetting unkindness.

If only the grave can calm us:
If there my bones and my brother's
Lying in peace, united,
Bring no reproach on the mother
Nor stir the father to anger:

Let us go down together,
Having despaired of wisdom:
The earth is as fruitful as ever,
The sea still teeming with fishes,
The sun still lusty; but we
Have failed to love, and must perish.

THE END OF FEAR

When a man has cast out fear
All is indifferent, and dear.

When desire has fled away
Then the little mice can play.

Leaning against the cedar's bark,
Or on a bear's neck in the dark,

Or lying in the mighty grass,
He is saved from what he was.

He can lay his head upon
Another's bosom, or a stone,

And the stone is well beloved,
And the breast by love unmoved:

The flesh uncursed and the stone blest,
The breast a stone, the stone a breast.

THE MOUNTAINOUS COUNTRY

1

Rain and the rainbow in the mountainous country:
There by the fall, at the ship's bows, in the mane of the wave
Arches the iris, and there in the foam prismatic
Bloom in an instant the seven colours in primitive purity:
There in the danger, in too much water, in the black valley.

The rain driving, the sun blooming, look back for the wonder;
Nothing is there but cloud clinging to breasts of the mountain,
To death's glistening bastions weakly clinging and weeping.
Walk out from the weeping, and look back when the rain ceases:
You were standing wrapped in the rainbow, in the mountainous
    country.

2

No harder lies the newborn head
In this dire valley than in lands
Where the long loamy levels spread
And give themselves into men's hands.

Fairer the trustful slumber seems
Beneath the hanging precipice,
Or the eternal-plunging streams
That thunder from the field of ice:

And destined to that dreadful sea,
Or the lean, little field that lies
Under the heel of tempest, he
Is master of their mysteries.

3

I depart far from myself into this land:
Lulled by the slow ship's deliberate drive
Leave both myself and you, and understand
A little how these silent people live,
Where water is the blessing and the curse;
Where water, from the high snows to the sea,
Makes a terrific universe
Of danger, and so sets the spirit free.
I muse, void as a vessel on the shore
At ebb-tide, blessed by mere emptiness
And sun and wind: and then once more

Comes the returning wave with bitter stress,
The endless conflict and the sighing sound;
And I must leave this anchorage and go
Onward to the far port where I am bound,
Through all the nights of storm and floes of ice
Between lost Eden and hoped Paradise.

4

The train will fight to the pass and pierce the mountains, or perish.
It has eaten holes in the rocks and leaped the ravines,
Banked up the gradients with the debris of its own onslaught,
Clamped down the bursting fall under titanic arches,
Covered itself with a roof of shields in the Roman manner,
Flung out huge fences like hands that shove away snowdrifts,
Fought with great charges of dynamite; and has conquered.
There was no greed of gain; the need of the people
Drove the terrific creature through the mountainous country.
It is their triumph, and a true emblem of honour.

O COME OUT OF THE LILY

O come out of the lily to me,
Come out of the morning-glory's bell,
Out of the rose and the peony,
You that made them, made so well
Leaf and flower and the spiral shell,
And the weed that waves in coves of the sea.

O look out of the ermine's eye,
And look down with the eye of the bird,
And ride the air with the butterfly
Whose wings are written with many a word,
Read and beloved but never heard,
The secret message, the silent cry.

116

O leap out of another's mind,
Come from the toils of the terrible brain:
Sleep no longer, nor lurk behind
Hate and anger and woeful pain:
As once in the garden, walk again,
Centre and spirit of human kind.

THE CHIMNEYPIECE

A painting by "AE", a goblet of shells sent from the Great Barrier Reef by Nettie Palmer, and a Christmas drawing by M. Rothenstein.

I look up, and there are three
Children wading in from sea,
And the foreign shells that were sent to me
And the little drawing of Charity.

Three painted children in the heat,
With sun-blessed heads and wave-blessed feet;
The cold shells, grey and violet,
And the drooped head in the snowy street.

Waters of birth blooming with light,
The water-forms, fulfilled with right,
Fair-tinted, or complete in white;
And pity's gift in the wan night.

Here may the Scorpion quench his sting
In his own watery brain, and sing
Like Swan or Siren voyaging
Through a dim thing to a far thing.

I that am born must come to be
Right as are the shells from sea;
And the bitter snow is calling me
To come through sorrow to charity.

THE SPRING

Where is the spring of my delight,
Now every spring is dry?
There is no blossom in my sight,
No sun is in the sky:

The birds are still and love is past,
And danger whistles shrill,
And life itself now looks aghast
And birth becomes an ill:

And yet the spring of my delight
Leaps up beyond belief,
As if it sprang in very spite –
In very spite of grief:

And yet the secret stream of grace
Flows on, and swells the same,
As if from out another place
Where sorrow has no name.

THE BUSH-BABY

I would rather hold this creature in my hand
Than be kissed by a great king.
The love for what I do not understand
Goes from me to the slight thing.

The moth-velvet and the round nocturnal eyes
And the unchanging face
Are excellent as an image out of Paradise,
As a flower in a dark place.

There is only mutual inoffensiveness
Between us, and a sense
Here in my heart, of what it is to bless
A simple immanence;

To see a glory in another kind,
To love, and not to know.
O if I could forsake this weary mind
And love my fellows so!

OLD, CHILDLESS, HUSBANDLESS

Old, childless, husbandless, bereaved, alone,
She knew more love than any I have known.
Familiar with the sickness at its worst,
She smiled at the old woman she had nursed
So long; whose bed she shared, that she might hear
The threadbare whisper in the night of fear.
She looked, and saw the change. The dying soul
Smiled her last thanks, and passed. Then Mary stole
About the room, and did what must be done,
Unwilling, kind heart, to call anyone,
It was so late: all finished, down she lay·
Beside the dead, and calmly slept till day.

Urania! what could child or husband be
More than she had, to such a one as she?

LAMENT FOR THE LANDLESS

In the dark by the bay-tree, by the noble laurel,
Haunted by rustling song-birds who come to rest
Like poems remembered, lodged in the leaves of honour,
Love of the earth leaps up, and falls in a sigh for my fellows.

Now it is winter, but some cold grapes linger:
Alas for the man who has never smelled the thick-flowering
Vine in its bursting glory, uniting the violet,
Rose, orange, lily and cyclamen, with the strength of yeast working,
The breath of the mighty sap labouring hugely.

Alas for the disinherited, the earthless, the uprooted –
No crocus, no primrose, no blessing of natural increment!
The flower of the plum hanging across the young moon
And the hedge-sparrow's brood with buttercup-yellow gullets
Are ravished from him, and he is a city of sorrows.

The beautiful strawberry and the decent violet growing together,
The pearl with the purple, the scarlet clasped in the green,
And lying among them the hopeful, the azure crescent
Of the half-eggshell, flung off by the life emerging
And cast by the careful mother beyond her dwelling:
Who is forlorn of these is the godforsaken.

Fair as the violet hangs the dark blue damson;
Few, but of gold, are the leaves that glitter about it;
Graceful the yellow mirabelle, the blonde darling,
Hangs down the arching twig dropped like the April grass-blade:
One season has laid on the gage that lichen-patina
Rich as your ancient bronzes: the great-limbed cherry
Stars with the seeds of burning her night of leafage.

There is fruit in the darkness of the massy ivy:
The caverned and shaggy ash-tod was heaped with its blossom
And hazy with wings, and murmuring with flies in October;
And now in the weak noon sun, in the crumbling hollow,
Stands large-eyed and dappled the lordly stormcock, the stag-bird,
Pen y llyn, cropping the inky knots of the plant of Bacchus.

Gratitude leaps and falls, and spreads into resignation.
I eat of the fruit of the tree where the good dog lies
Meshed in the quiet root, and my hand is busy
On wrinkled stems that were planted by the forgotten;
And I must be numbered with them and neglect the seasons,
Though somehow I know that a flower is remembered for ever,
And eyes, and the shape of a bird, for ever remembered.

But the bride, and the plant of the heart, is the wheat in the valleys.
In May; when the virgin ear is adust, and the swallows
Shoot like the darts of love through airs of delight,
Heaven is on earth, and every creature proclaims it.
The wind in the wheat is the breath of the breast of my mother,
And the holy corn in the ear is my true love's posy.[1]

THE FISHERS

The embattled towers, the level lilied moat,
Between the lily-leaves the inverted sky,
The impending alders and the quivering float
Charmed the vexed spirit, and it was not I,
But contemplating essence that surveyed
The brightness, and the water, and the shade.

There stole two silent children to my side,
And sat down with a still attentive air;
The elder thin, and dark, and dignified,
The younger smiling, five years old, and fair:
Quietly as the ousel and the wren
They bore themselves, for they were fishermen.

[1] The last nine words are borrowed from a North Sea chanty.

121

Despite their wounded trousers and their knees
Calloused with wear, I could not think them boys,
(Creatures who shatter all the summer's ease,
Whooping like furies, born to rhyme with noise);
Composed and courteous beings, full of grace,
They seemed the quiet spirits of the place.

The elder fixed his quick black wild-duck eye
Far in the depths, to watch for the great pike:
The younger looked and murmured blissfully
At waterfowl and cranefly and the like,
Naming the dabchick, and with eye intent
Pointing with snail-horn finger where she went.

And turning to the meadow in the sun
Smiled at three mares in the dim whitethorn shade;
Blessed them like Adam in the new-begun
World, when the immemorial names were made:
Like Adam innocent, like Adam fond,
He whispered, *Blossom, Sweetheart, Diamond.*

His fellow brooded like a child of stone,
Yet not unhappy: he was touched by care,
And care accepted; that grave union
Of virtues that the travelling soul must wear,
Decent compunction, strong philosophy,
Showed like the sign of a brave man to be.

Such were these fishers; one in love with all
That fell beneath his soft enamoured look,
And one in search of the old magical
Surcease and silver healing of the brook;
Friends, though asunder; and (I saw them then
With Izaak's eye), Anglers, and honest men.

And the tall flower was peace made visible,
The air was ambient love; the flashing fly
Was the soul's dear mysterious parable,
Proclaiming the immortal silently;
And sweetest kindness sat beneath the trees
In two unasked, affectionate presences.

Good children, I am glad we made no kill;
That would have tarnished what I felt for you.
Two gentle souls, in whom was nothing ill,
Looked from the dark eye and the dreaming blue,
Where by the water and the tower of might
The hurt healed, and the mind was filled with light.

THE SAINT'S PROGRESS

(From an early Italian painting)

Through the poplar-steepled plain
And the terraced, tangled vine,
Up the hill-path serpentine
To the mountain veiled in rain,
To the high place of the goat,
Shuddering to the eagle's throat;
More than fearless, gay and fair
Trips the Saint, whose candid dress
Makes the ragged wilderness
Clear and courtly, and whose hair
Is as bright and clean and neat
As the buskins on his feet,
Shoes supernal, which no stain
Gather on the ghastly way,
Which the stone can never fray,
Which essay no steep in vain.

At the summit, O what sight
Greets the child arrayed in white!
The old, grey, unforgiving sea,
And the alien lands afar,
The island where the dragons are,
And dim with dreadful mystery
Furthest from his gentle home,
The spiring smoke of martyrdom!

He beholds it all, with eyes
Eager still, and undismayed;
Faithful, courteously arrayed,
Still he hastens, still he flies;
The flower he plucked this morning new
Has not lost its pearl of dew,
But is smiling in his face
While he dances to the shore
Gaily, then is seen no more,
As he passes on his race
Swiftly to the final place.

THE BIRD IN THE TREE

That tree, and its haunting bird,
        Are the loves of my heart;
But where is the word, the word,
        O where is the art,

To say, or even to see,
        For a moment of time,
What the tree and the Bird must be
        In the true sublime?

They shine, they sing to the soul,
    And the soul replies;
But the inner love is not whole,
    And the moment dies.

O give me before I die
    The grace to see
With eternal, ultimate eye,
    The Bird and the Tree.

The song in the living green,
    The Tree and the Bird –
O have they ever been seen,
    Ever been heard?

BLOWETH WHERE IT LISTETH

My ghost goes about while I stay here,
Like any wandering moth it flits abroad in air;
Seeking the unsought, and loving what is lone,
The cloudy-minded poor, and the weed by the cold stone:
The frail bird that summons life to fill the ragged nest,
And the woman who has no words to ease her burdened breast.

My spirit flew over, and lifted up its hand
Above the yellow ragweed growing in the poor cold land,
Over the lonely yarrow nodding in the rain,
Till it came to a cottage in a solitary lane,
Where the sparrow, nested in the neighbouring tree,
Brooded the shabby eggs which no one loved but she.

My ghost looked in at the window, and saw a poor soul
Sprinkling the linen with water from a bowl,
Putting on the kettle to boil for the tea,
Then taking up the flat-iron, and ironing diligently:
And my ghost peered in anxiously, to mark the look of care,
But for once in this sorry life sorrow was not there.

Sorrow had been there, but it was fled away;
She was all alone, but it was her joyful day;
There lurked about her lip a tremulous smile and fond
As she glanced through the window into the lane beyond,
And absently and tenderly beheld the shabby tree
Where the sparrow hugged the eggs which no one loved but she.

My ghost flew away, and it was well content,
For it took her tenderness with it as it went:
For it goes about blessing, and will not be gainsaid,
The wild weed in the waste land, the ruined wall and the dead;
And the hearts of poor women in the cold countryside
It goes about blessing, and will not be denied.

CIDER IN THE POTTING-SHED

I'm sitting in the Potting-shed
    Listening to the rain.
The tiles are streaming overhead,
    The garden breathes again:
The summer cabbages outside
    Are drumming to the drops,
So here will you and I abide
    And drink until it stops.

I'll sit upon this heap of mould,
    You on that pile of sand,
And each of us shall firmly hold
    A tankard in his hand.
And so that neither one shall be
    Disturbed or put about,
The boy who brought the cider, he
    Shall stand and pour it out.

And here's your bit of bread and cheese,
    And here likewise is mine.
Look at the bloomy Apple-trees,
    They twinkle and they shine;
The rainbow is above the wood
    Beyond the garden wall,
And near and far, in solitude,
    The Maytime cuckoos call.

THE RUDE POTATO

By jobbing Jimmy this was found
Last autumn, as he delved the ground
To get the late potatoes up
And save the nice clean heavy crop.
He saw it was irregular,
As these large tubers often are;
A second glance convincèd old Jas.
Just how irregular it was.
Comic potatoes do occur,
But in the life of Jimmy Burr
Who's handled many score of tons
And spotted all the funny ones,
This was the rudest he had met.
Its shamelessness was quite complete,
Warming the honest gardener's heart
By asking no least touch of art,
Which nearly all such gems require
To make them apt to our desire.

No nugget of the purest ore
Could have delighted Jimmy more.
A slow, profound, and spreading grin
Proclaimed the gratitude within:
Then on a handy frame he laid

The treasure, and resumed the spade –
Or stay – no doubt resumed the fork,
Which is more usual for such work.

Emerging from the kitchen door
Comes Mitzi (from the Danube shore)
For parsley, or some subtler weed
Such as these foreign artists need.
She spots the tuber on the frame,
And stops to scrutinise the same.
Then O what peals of peasant mirth
Explode above our chilly earth!
She shrieks, bends double, beats her thighs;
She clasps her sides; then wipes her eyes
To get another look, and then
She has gone off in fits again.
And all the day, when here and there
She has a little time to spare,
She comes; and one refreshing peep
Such dews of joy can make her weep,
That all her sorrows seem to fade,
And glee transforms the exiled maid.
Hark! as she dishes up, she sings
What sound like wild Danubian things;
And later, at the fall of night,
"Roll Out the Barrel" *almost* right.

Fain would she keep the glorious thing,
That makes a lonely exile sing:
But Jimmy takes it, when he goes
To taste the nectar at the "Rose
And Crown", when all our worthies are
Gathered at evening in the bar.
The slighter spirits yell with glee
The freakish masterpiece to see,
But stately Drake, the landlord, winks
At Jimmy Burr above the drinks,
And gravely hangs the wonder up
For all to see who take a cup,

Then gives old Jim two ten-bob notes,
Which go to slake the assembled throats.
"That's Nature!" says imposing Drake:
"Now, gentlemen, what will you take?"

O Science! can you make us mirth
Like this dull apple of the earth?
And what in art can do us good
Like this, so nourishing, so lewd?
Only by life such joy is lent,
Wild, bracing, and inconsequent.

GARDENERS ALL

There is no race, no tribe of man,
No type, no class, no clique, no clan,
No colour, caste, religion, age,
Free from the Gardener's sacred rage.
So thought I, when of late I went
Into that vast cathedral-tent
Where annually, when times allow,
Such roaring tides of Gardeners flow.
And by a Gardener I mean
One who delights in all that's green;
(Save the worst weeds) and in whose face
Love to the vegetable race
Glows like a beacon, when he sees
Fair, useful plants and pleasant trees.
I do not condescend to sing
Those for whom gardens are the thing;
Who think, because they merely spend,
They have attained a proper end;
Who will not see and will not know
Aught save the highlights of the show –
The personage with miles of grounds
And "novelties" at several pounds.

No! First, as in his rightful place,
Let Parson stand and say our grace.
Tall, rangy, with great sunburned hands,
He mountaineered in many lands,
And fell in love, long years ago,
With those small angels of the snow,
The Alpines, in whose fairy bells
And minion leaves perfection dwells.
Of course he has to grow a lot
Of kitchen stuff to fill the pot,
Sweet-peas and roses, willy-nilly,
And for the altar many a lily.
But given a half-hour free of trouble
You'll see his lofty form bent double
Above the small moraine and scree
And alp, which form his rockery.
He climbs by stooping, and his crown
In life is won by looking down.

That lady, with the nervous air,
Notebook, and specs, and wispy hair,
To whom exhibitors defer,
Making a mighty fuss of her,
Is she who raised a foreign weed
From a mere pinch of hard-won seed,
Crossed and selected, rogued and saved
Till phalanxes of colour waved
All over Europe, and a new
Beauty had blazed upon our view.
Under that squashy hat, what will,
What science, and what practised skill!
Maiden herself, she is the queen
(In one department) of the Gene.

How different, among old maids,
Is yonder she in pastel shades,
Who cultivates a flowery soul,
And in a blossom sees the Whole!
No March will find the daffodil

Absent from her town window-sill.
She has a country cottage too,
All bowered up in pink and blue,
Round which she wanders starry-eyed
To find where early violets hide.
She has a herb-garden, and store
Of books on old-world garden lore;
Puts lavender in little bags
For Yule-tide sale to other hags,
And she is always stewing simples
To dab upon her curls and dimples.
She asks young men to tea (the lambs!)
And offers them her home-made jams,
Astonishing their callow minds
By serving up unheard of kinds,
In which repulsive things are blent
By way of gay experiment.
Dear lady, take a tip from me!
They all prefer good Strawberry.
She cons the lily and the rose,
But little of herself she knows;
If she could analyse her mind,
How staggered she would be to find
Lurking beneath her starry eye
A Tyrant of the deepest dye!

Here, looking just a little sad,
(Most men of fifty do) is Dad,
Eyeing the roses with an air
Like the faint ghost of love's despair.
To such a pass romantics come
After they've been and married Mum,
And youthful dreams must go repose
Under their monument, the rose.
Perverse old Dad! you've got a wife
Who is a cushion to your life,
Housekeeps so well, and mends, and cooks,
Is kind, and not so bad for looks;
And such a mother! where could be

A batch of kids to beat your three?
But still the old unsatisfied
Visions within the heart abide;
And since you are not really bad,
No wicked, dissipated Dad;
Since you don't reason much, nor wholly
Identify your melancholy,
Love's face has dreamed itself into
This perfect Rose, a queen to you.

That stalwart form and ruddy face
Which *make simplicity a grace*,
Belong to Bill, the railwayman,
Who does as much as mortal can
With runner beans, and roots, and peas,
At Umpteen Railway Cottages,
And whose untiring efforts shine
At various points along the line.
Each likely bush in shape he lops,
Grows rhubarb by the buffer-stops,
In scarlet salvia, like a flame,
Writes Nether Wopsall's glorious name
Above the platform, and will put
Something wherever flowers can shoot.
On warm midsummer eves I meet
Him homeward bound with burden sweet,
Delicious pinks, which William grows
On his allotment-ground in rows.
But his abiding passion seems
Towards the Parsnip of his dreams,
For which the aspirant unblenching
Must do a lot of solid trenching;
And then at sowing-time he must
Take sifted soil as fine as dust,
Make crowbar-holes to fill with this,
Then sow the awkward seed in threes.
If faithfully he shall attend
The plants, he will attain his end –
A bunch of roots like cream-laid paper,

Full two feet long, and smooth and taper,
Which he rejoicing homeward brings,
And shows, or eats, the nasty things.[1]

See where good Bill enchanted stands,
With fixed blue eyes, and hanging hands,
Before the stand of Blank & Co.,
Whose veg-seeds are the Ones to Grow.
Whose root-crops all so clean and nice
Weary the mind with form precise;
Whose blushing Celery was dug
From land which never knew a slug;
Whose Marrow, Eggplant, Toms. and Cues
Dazzle the eye with various hues,
Whose Broc. and Cauli., Peas and Beans,
Sweet Corn and Waxpods, different Greens,
Are to our Bill a Pantheon, where
He feels both glory and despair.

And this tall Lady, who exhales
An atmosphere of knightly tales,
Moves, like the patroness of all,
With leisured paces through the hall.
Long discipline has so refined
In her, the movements of the mind,
That love she can no more express
Save as an ambient graciousness,
And anger as a numbing chill,
Dreadful to him who does the ill.
In her reside most subtle powers
Which she sets forth in terms of flowers,
Seeking the strangest; and this art
Is the rare language of her heart.
She feels her order doomed; and she,
The lingering bloom of chivalry,
Writes thus her hymn to death, too proud,
Too wise to voice her pain aloud.

[1] No, they are not nasty when intelligently cooked.

Where everyone is frank and nice,
Whose are those nasty furtive eyes,
That slinking form which never stands
Still, and those skinny restless hands,
Unlike the paws of pleasant brown
Which all our honest Gardeners own?
It is the horrid Pincher, who
Invades the sacred groves of Kew,
And who will take, if take he can,
A costly plant from any man.
The rare, small Alpines he prefers,
Or, as he goes from bad to worse,
Into a hothouse he will slip
And some sleek pseudo-bulb will nip.
Of course I do not mean to call
This blot a Gardener at all:
For what he steals, the shiftless wretch
Sells for whatever it will fetch
To shady coves, or else to mugs,
In pubs where there are nasty fugs.
The creature never tills the soil,
Nor could endure such honest toil;
So we must watch, if we are wise,
This serpent in our Paradise,
Classing him as a garden pest
With wireworm, greenfly, and the rest,
And spraying him, whenever seen,
With winter-wash or Paris green.

But lo, the Monarch of the show!
Our Mr Mackintosh, you know.
Tyrannic as the eastern wind,
But king of all the gardening kind.
I think that there is no one here,
No scientist, no gardener,
Could find the man at fault at all
In matters horticultural.
Land him at fifteen thousand feet,
His botany would be complete;

So would it be within a mine
Where hoary Moulds and Fungi shine.
Each soil, however rare, he knows,
From clinging clay to sand that blows,
And answers up both sharp and sure
To any question on manure.
No hitch in heating need he fear,
For he's a first-rate engineer,
And quickly deals with huge amounts,
In costs, and wages, and accounts.
Men say that every single worm
In land belonging to his firm,
Is noted by his piercing looks
And duly entered in his books.
The pests with him have little chance,
For greenfly withers at his glance,
And codlin-moths fall from the air
And perish, if he does but swear;
Not that he often swears; his eye
Serves him so well with man or fly.

Yet mark that granite optic now,
For he has paused before a row
Of rarest Lilies; and behold,
There is a new one, greenish gold,
Of form ethereal, habit fine,
And perfume like a noble wine.
Now he expands, he truly lives.
He does not use superlatives,
But one may see a light arise,
A glow shine from the granite eyes.
Scarcely a rocky feature moves,
But there he stands, and looks, and loves.

THE WEED

Don't pull me up! I got to live,
The same as what you got to do,
And uman people never give
A thought to what a weed goes through –
Unted and acked and oed to death
We ardly dror a peaceful breath.

I dessay now you love your Mum,
And mind the things she as to say:
Don't think of me as thievin scum –
I'm a good daughter in my way;
There ain't a plant, there ain't a grass
A better weed than Mother was.

Er figger was a sight to see!
So round and full in the rosette;
And then er way – so bright and free,
Takin what umus she could get,
And when our earts was in our boots
Sayin "Cheer up! you got your roots!"

She ad er roots all right, ad Ma,
As Tom the gardener's boy could tell;
E said they reached Australia,
And sometimes that they went to – well,
E'd lug the tops off poor old Mum,
But in a fortnight up she'd come.

She knew the ropes, did Mum, all right.
"Grow near some borjwar plant," she'd say,
"What's like yourself, and ide from sight
Till everyone's on oliday,
Then bloom at such a crackin pace
That weeds will fill the blinkin place!"

And ow my Mum did 'ate the plants
You silly people love to grow,
And ow she did egg on the ants
To muck their roots up from below,
The wireworms and the capsid bugs –
And ow she lectured them old Slugs!

"You boys can get about", says she;
"Good Lor! if I could do the same,
I wouldn't leave a single tree,
Or any veg. what's worth the name;
I'm sick of all the lot of you,
The bits of damage what you do!

Go on! ave them carnations down!
Climb up them roses and them beans!
Spit on them lilies, turn 'em brown,
And show what reverlootion means!
One good night's work ud wreck the show!
Ooray, me brave lads! orf you go!"

Them slugs they never stopped to think!
They all come out from underground,
And lumme! they ad all turned pink,
And made a norrid flappin sound
Like dishrags blowin overead,
They run so fast at what she said!

And all the night we eard em munch,
And all night long we eard em chew;
At first the ole outrageous bunch,
And then we only eard a few;
At last, O orrors! we eard pops,
And then a lot of flabby flops.

At lenth there came the gashly dawn –
And we could see, on every side,
Their pore white bodies on the lawn;
And on the paths, split open wide
Was them dead eroes that ad bust
To wreck the garden Mum ad cussed!

Pore Mum she shivered, and the dew
Fell off er flowers like angel's tears;
She says, "I bin the death of you,
That was such good ardworkin dears;
And there you lay like bits of dough!
Not bloomin well for nothing, though!"

And then she drored erself up straight –
I never see er look so fine –
And bellered, "Thus we demonstrate
The will of weeds as is divine!
Ow richly they ave earned their rests
To win the world for weeds and pests!"

But Mum she never moped for long;
She shook erself and stretched er shoots,
And swelled er buds out big and strong,
And felt about with all er roots,
Tryin er best to make quite sure
No garden plant should get manure.

Oh, it was lovely when a bee
Come to Mum's flowers and made er giggle;
Of course it was all Greek to me,
But I just loved to see er wriggle:
And once I said, "Mum, are bees nice?"
I ad no chance to say it twice!

She turned on me like anything!
"You nasty dirty little cat!
You must a bin philanderin
With bees, to say a thing like that!
Such words from me own flesh and blood
Before you've even got a bud!"

Of course I understand it now,
For Mum she told me, later on,
That bees what come when flowers blow
Are like a weddin to each one,
And ow she thought a peony
Ad bin the pa of Sis and me.

And we must old our eads up igh,
Because we was not common weeds,
And grow like anything, and try
To make the most of all our seeds;
But 'ate the posh flowers just the same,
Because they grudged us poor pa's name.

I ope I shall repay er trust,
And not forget er lovely words,
Nor them eroic slugs what bust
And left their bodies to the birds;
It elps in all our goins on
To think of loved ones as is gone.

For our dear Ma she is no more!
I never shall forget the day
When Mr Thompson raged and swore,
And said e'd turn young Tom away
For leaving weeds as big as Mum
And letting lots of others come.

The boy e muttered something rude,
And moaned a bit about is wrongs,
And ow e was misunderstood –
Then fetched a fork with orrid prongs,
A basket, and a nasty spud,
And said e'd ave our mother's blood!

Jab went the fork – it turned me bad,
E stuck it in so far below
Poor Mum – a gruntin from the lad
I eard – I eard er taproot go!
Er roots laid naked in the sun!
E'd got the lot – poor Ma was done.

E flung er on is orrid eap,
To wither all the long day through,
But all the time poor Mum would keep
Calling to us; although she knew
She was a goner, yet she tried
To keep our earts up till she died.

All the ot day she called and said,
"E missed you young uns, glory be!
You'll be alive when I am dead,
So don't you go and grieve for me!
Take all the umus you can get!
Suckers and seeds! we'll beat em yet!"

Suckers and seeds! the weeds will win!
We'll get the ole world for our own!
Then Oh ow glorious will come in
The era of the great Self-sown!
Ave you the eart to kill me now,
After my touchin story?... OW!!!

OTHER PEOPLE'S GLASSHOUSES

While gazing round this dear ramshackle one
(Not even my own, but which I help to run),
I think of what such pleasances can be,
And dream of them in tender reverie.
Those which begin with excavated sites,
Well reared with brick foundations, pressed-steel lights,
The latest heating, cunning ventilation,
Water laid on, and kind anticipation
Of all a tender plant can well demand;
With all the stores laid ready to the hand
Of richest turfy loam, manure, and peat,
Sand, sphagnum, oakleaf-mould so dark and sweet,
With stacks of clean red pots and labels white,
And every ware to forward the delight.
I muse, and faintly hope that one glad day
Some genial Duke or great rich man will say
"We have some Glass which you may like to see;
It will not bore you? Good! Then follow me."
(Note that the Duke but grows to please himself,
Perhaps for shows, but not for sordid pelf;
So no Tomato-vistas I expect,
Nor endless Cucumbers, nor those erect
Chrysanths disbudded to but one a plant,
Which markets, but not Christians, seem to want.)

The Duke, so portly in his ancient tweeds,
Crosses a yard designed for glasshouse needs:
My eye, already ravished, straight begins
To dote on potting-sheds and compost-bins,
Remarks a fruit-store, and yet always keeps
Reverting to the stables' juicy heaps;
Nor can I well contain the envious sigh
Where scores of tons of leaf-mould tower high.

But of these background joys I say no more;
The Duke is beckoning from an open door,
Through which appear Azaleas' dawny hues,

The starry Cinerarias' endless blues,
Rare Primulas, far-gathered from the snows
From which they rear their coronets of rose,
By stout adventurers, who boldly face
Strange Lamas, and the savage holy place,
To win the trophy of enchanting grace:
Ranks of Carnations, to all ladies dear,
Of whose sweet taste I write approval here,
For these pre-eminent myself I think,
As long as you don't overdo the pink.

Another door – a damp delicious heat,
Odours half sinister, or languid-sweet,
And glistening pseudo-bulbs and strangest flowers
Stand massed in pans, or else depend in showers.
The Orchid-House! where all my being owns
A deep delight; where these my northern bones
Thaw, and the frugal cautious northern eye,
Abandoned to a tropic revelry,
Gazes its hungry fill; the northern nose
Its usual criterion, the rose,
Forgets awhile, and sniffs exotic scent
With large expansion and profound content;
While the incorrigible northern mind
Ponders the wonder of the orchid kind,
And though enchanted has a corner free
To marvel at their strange biology.

Forward, to where in borders, pots and tubs
Stand sturdy and delicious Trees and Shrubs!
Well-dressed Camellias flourish with the Bay,
Which is as stately, not so bright as they.
Glorious Camellias, whose hardy green
Defies our winter, and whose flowers are seen
Crowding in February, rich and fair,
When all our native shrubs are poor and bare;
And here, where they are sheltered, flower at will,
Though snow be drifted up on every sill.

Ye simple gardeners, why do you not grow
This vigorous Beauty which delights us so?

But look where Orange-trees in fruit and bud
Bless our cold eyes, and stir nostalgic blood
To pine, as ever, for their odorous groves,
Their fireflies, and their Mediterranean loves!
The poets' Myrtle, now so seldom seen,
With small spiced bloom and neat and sober green;
The glorious Fuchsia (call it Farthingale),
So fair in every kind from dark to pale,
So neat, so perfect; could a gardener want
A lovelier object, or a kindlier plant?
And ranging round, the genial showman comes
To his own favourites, the Geraniums,
(And, I confess it, favourites of mine,
So do not call the Duke a Philistine).
Not in small pots, but in the border, these
Ascend a trellis, and are tall as trees:
Bright, clear, and simple, easy to content,
At home in palace or in tenement,
Sumptuous, scented, flowering so long,
Dear to the heart, if not renowned in song.

And in this Shrub-house there are sure to be
Some curious things from far beyond the sea,
Such rarities as roving uncles seek:
Many uncommon, one or two unique;
Some gifts of princes, some of gardening aunts;
But all are notable and wondrous plants.

And now the Duke has left the Shrubs, and flits
Stately but eager past the forcing-pits,
To show the lean-to where his Fig-tree spreads
A solemn, large-leaved shade above our heads.
Grave, reverend plant! its leaden limbs are smooth,
The thoughtful eye and loving hand to soothe,
And the rich sober fruit can take the mind
Back to old Vergil and his worthy kind.

143

Long could I sit beneath this solemn tree,
Well entertained with thoughts of piety;
Likening good men to this fruit, with skin
Of modest hue, but bright and sweet within.

Now my enthusiastic Mentor reaches
The fair abode of Nectarines and Peaches,
Whose gracile twigs, with willowy leaves, are tied
Neat to the well-spaced wire on either side,
While their rich burdens, red or golden-pale,
Delicious breathings on the air exhale,
So that we seem absolved from sin and woe,
And Adam's curse is lifted, as we go
Wandering slowly in delicious ease
Along this blessed colonnade of trees,
Forgetting fortune and our different birth,
And only thankful that we walk the earth:
Lose Adam's curse in Adam's primal right,
Strangely absolved by mutual delight!

But let me not too selfishly impose
On my kind host, who may have gouty toes.
The Melons and the Mushrooms I will pass
And all the other glories of the glass.
I will forgo even the lordly Pines,
If I may thoroughly inspect – the Vines!
Ah sacred sight, the grand symbolic Plant,
Assuaging many a deep-felt human want,
Filling the eye with beauty, and the mind
With old associations deep and kind,
Ay, solemn too; which for the body's use
Distils that peerless and poetic juice,
So evident a blessing from above,
Whoso rejects it, him I cannot love.

Here let me wander, seeking till I find
Of the whole race the one, the peerless kind.
Not the Black Hamburg, though full well I know
This is the best for such as I to grow,

For in ramshackle houses with no heat
The willing creature ripens black and sweet:
Not the *Gross* Colmar, though this be so much
Grown for the market by the clever Dutch;
Not Canon Hall, for though 'tis large and fair
The flavour is too often wanting there.
For but a lingering moment I survey
The sweet, delicious, but too small Tokay,
But from the whole Sweetwater tribe escape –
Their flavour is unworthy of the grape;
And all the other kinds I wander by,
All good, yet only one can satisfy.
Ah! here at last we find its shy retreat;
A special Span or Dome, with extra heat.

Take the whole garden, friend, but leave me this,
The Alexandrian Muscat, plant of bliss,
With long and taper bunches hanging down,
(The best and ripest darkening into brown),
Which cracked society's capricious flukes
Deny to poets, and concede to dukes!
Whose savour reconciles the glee of youth
With the grave mellowness of heavenly truth;
Which when I taste, perception seems to be
Translated into purest poetry,
My griefs transfigured to supernal gold,
At once by nature and by art consoled.

The Duke will read my longing in my eyes,
With ready secateur will sympathise;
And while we munch, I know we shall agree
On Progress and Perfectibility;
For none can disbelieve the promised bliss,
Or immortality, while tasting this.
The Alexandrian in fruit or flower
Forbids impiety, or lust for power;
And where he shoots, to man there are restored
Some ells of Eden: here the flaming sword

Is sheathed; those Sentinels so dread and bright
Sit down with us, and share in our delight....

Vain vision! when the changing world each day
Sees some such lordly pleasance pass away;
When the mere stripling knows my symbols all
Worn tokens, heaven hypothetical,[1]
Nature indifferent, and the dreams of men
Figments of longing which we must condemn.
Yet keep these plants, O Man! a kindlier time
May yet be moved by them to better rhyme,
Or moved, like me, to place his pleasure low,
On the firm Earth, whence Men and Blossoms grow.

[1] To say the least.

A PERFECT LOT OF LETTUCE

So timely sown and timely thinned,
    The soil so nicely hoed,
A sheltered place, a season kind,
    Love round them as they growed:

They hearted up by Whitsuntide,
    Though done in open ground
And Whitsun early; how my pride
    And pleasure did abound.

No blasted slugs nor wireworm came,
    Nor any frost did strike;
As clean as in a house, or frame,
    They stood there all alike.

The village housewives came with pleas,
　　And offered handsome pay
To have them for the hikers' teas
　　On Whitsun holiday.

I stood and hesitated long;
　　To pull them seemed a shame;
For why? when only one was gone
　　They would not look the same.

But there, the stuff was grown to eat,
　　We should be thankful of it,
So let the hikers have their treat
　　And cottage wives their profit.

They must be pulled, or run to seed.
　　We will not let it fret us.
But I'll remember till I'm dead
　　That perfect lot of lettuce.

RHUBARB PIE

or The Rival Pastrycooks

Kids are funny! you never know
How to take them. I had to go
Up to London the other day,
So I asked my neighbour across the way
To give them all their dinner, see?
She's always very kind to me.
So she agreed like, quite content;
I packed my bag and off I went.
And when I got back, pretty late,
I said to my twin girls, what's eight,
"Now Dawn and Eve", I said, "come on,
And tell me all you been and done.

147

I hope that you were very good,
And nicely-mannered with your food,
And that young Charl and little Dave
And Peter didn't misbehave.
I'm certain sure that Mrs Price
Took pains to cook you something nice;
Not like your own mum, but she'd try."
They said, "Chop toad, and roobub pie".
"What, roobub pie, what you can't eat?
I'll have to pop across the street
And tell her that you can't abide
Puddns and pies with that inside.
Oh dear, she would be vexed, I know,
To see you go and leave it so."

"But Mum", they said, "we ate a lot!
It was so nice, and fresh, and hot!
We said to Mrs Price, O my,
This is a lovely Roobub Pie!"

Well, well, I thought, this is a change!
On Sunday, when I light the range,
To do the roast, and Monday's stew,
I'll make a Roobub Pie or two.

D'you think they'd touch it? Oh dear no!
They sat the whole five in a row;
They sat and looked me in the eye.
They said, "We don't like Roobub Pie"!!!
And goodness knows the reason why!

THE DIEHARDS

We go, in winter's biting wind,
On many a short-lived winter day,
With aching back but willing mind
To dig and double-dig the clay.

All in November's soaking mist
We stand and prune the naked tree,
While all our love and interest
Seem quenched in blue-nosed misery.

We go in withering July
To ply the hard incessant hoe;
Panting beneath the brazen sky
We sweat and grumble, but we go.

We go to plead with grudging men,
And think it is a bit of luck
When we can wangle now and then
A load or two of farmyard muck.

What do we look for as reward?
Some little sounds, and scents, and scenes:
A small hand darting strawberry-ward,
A woman's apron full of greens.

A busy neighbour, forced to stay
By sight and smell of wallflower-bed;
The plum-trees on an autumn day,
Yellow, and violet, and red.

Tired people sitting on the grass,
Lulled by the bee, drugged by the rose,
While all the little winds that pass
Tell them the honeysuckle blows.

The sense that we have brought to birth
Out of the cold and heavy soil,
These blessed fruits and flowers of earth
Is large reward for all our toil.

A SUMMER DESSERT

The empty dish was fair,
Lofty, bordered with green.
We laid the vine-leaves there
With fronds of the fern between;
Black-currants' bold gypsy eyes,
Strings of the rubied red,
White of the largest size,
Like the eyes in our pale cat's head;
The beautiful Mirabelle,
Early, elegant, gold,
Disposed on the twig so well,
Made in the cherry's mould;
Two kinds of the Raspberry,
Soft yellow and bloomy rose,
The mountain Strawberry,
The prettiest thing that grows,
Plucked in sprays, with the white
Bud and blossom, and pale
Unripe fruit; our delight
Lived, and became a tale.
The picture dwelt in the mind,
The pleasure took root;
We triumphed when we combined
Our love with a dish of fruit.

THE MORALS OF PRUNING

When I, who stands as fate to this strong Vine,
Take up the steel, and the devoted shoot,
Not for its own felicity, but mine,
Eye sternly, and determined that the fruit
Is to be here and this, so much, no more –
I think of miseries that men deplore:

Their hopes curtailed, like the thinned cluster here:
Life interrupted, like this shortened stem;
Old certitudes removed, as when I shear
The gnarled unfruitful rods, and carry them
To the indifferent fire; such surgery
Life does upon my fellows, and on me.

If we could think our pain but part designed
By some such purpose as evokes this great
Delicious cluster, where we else should find
All wasteful and all trivial, then our fate
Might be absolved, and we more calmly grow;
At least they cannot prove it is not so.

THE BAY-TREE

Twenty feet high, and thirty feet about!
Such beauties are uncommon, there's no doubt;
And to have such a lordly thick-leaved Bay
In our bleak county, on the cold stiff clay!
How many an evening, when the fading light
Summons the gardener to the fireside bright,
And the cold clinging earth is scraped away
From spade and hoe, have I approached the Bay
To see the daily homecoming begin
Of birds, to whom this plant is as an inn;
Who in their gratitude for shelter keep

151

A time for song between their toil and sleep,
Who like the travellers of former time
Make their roof ring with roundelay and rhyme!
So loud they sing, so many sing, it seems
A tower of bells, a living church, whose limbs
So shake and tremble, that the dark-green spire
Seems with a triple life to be on fire;
One life its own, one for its thronging birds,
One for that anthem unperplexed by words.

FOR US ALL

It is the spring of the year and a cold morning.
It is a late spring too, and nothing wakes
Save the first primrose, hugging the moss she was born in,
And the pink-studded branch that the wind shakes,
Wafting the delicate colour down in flakes.

It is the spring of our time, the time for dying,
If hope is too heavy to lift and you cannot find
Strength to endure the east, see the petal flying,
To weather the last weeks and the most unkind
Of the whole winter, living upon the mind.

Side by side with the old joy and the old sorrow
We bear the unheard-of hope and the new pain.
Like winter wheat under the iron harrow
We grasp the soil and await the April rain;
Toil and endurance shall earn the harvest again.

ROMFORD MARKET

With human bellow, bovine blare,
Glittering trumpery, gaudy ware,
The life of Romford market-square
Set all our pulses pounding:
The gypsy drover with his stick,
The huckster with his hoary trick,
The pork with fat six inches thick
And sausages abounding:

Stalls of apples, stacks of cake,
Piles of kippers, haddocks, hake,
Great slabs of toffee that men make,
Which urchins eye and pray for:
Divine abundance! glorious day!
We stayed as long as we could stay,
Then upped our loads and went our way
With all that we could pay for.

And homeward bound by Clockhouse Lane
We jabbered of our golden gain,
And not in our too usual vein
Of rancorous dissension;
Here is the little onion-hoe
We bought that day so long ago;
Worn down – but so are one or two
More things that I could mention.

Threading the silent, mist-bedewed
And darkening thicks of Hainault Wood,
We reached that cottage, low and rude,
Which was so dear a dwelling;
By the black yew, solemn and still,
Under the brow of Crabtree Hill;
Ah, dear it was, and ever will
Be dear beyond all telling.

Dry hornbeam-twigs roared up in flame,
The kettle quivered to the same;
When home the weary parents came
The sausages were frying;
The tea was brewed, the toast was brown –
We chattered of our day in town;
Outside the leaves went whispering down,
And autumn owls were crying.

Our market-day was done. But we
Enshrine it still in memory,
For it was passed in perfect glee,
By youth and health begotten:
My Romford on the Essex plain,
My upland woods! while you remain
One humble jewel we retain,
One day is unforgotten.

AGAINST GREAT OLD QUICKSET
GARDEN HEDGES

You who have toiled with the shears
Years and years,
You who have fried in the sun
At the job that is never done –
Sixteen square feet to the one-foot run;
You who still groan and mutter
Even while the electric cutter
Clatters along the quick
(Six feet high, four feet thick)
Straining your arms and necks
And sometimes slicing its own flex:
What's it all for?
Don't do it any more!

Keeping the grass too wet to mow,
Piling up battlements of snow,
Full of dog-holes down below;
Full of nice nests,
Yes, but full of bad pests;
Topped with horrible old clumps
Which the swinked hedger leaves as bumps,
And various helpers, lads, friends, loafers,
Convert in time to things like sofas,
While sides and bottom are a shambles
Of elders, ivy, briers and brambles –
Before the frosty mornings flit
Up and have a bash at it!

Worm your way in.
Never mind about your skin.
However thick, however big,
Cut an entrance twig by twig,
Burrow to its secret maw,
Bare the stems, and use the saw.
Lug the matted masses out,
Burn the flimsy, save the stout!
Never mind the mess it makes –
Leave the headers, save the stakes!
Scrape the loamy bottom bare,
Look what treasure's hidden there!
A cricket-ball, a pipkin-lid,
The big stone jar some playboy hid,
Bikes and bedsteads, bits of wire,
Loads of dead stuff for the fire,
And lastly, worth its weight in gold,
Heaped between the hawthorns old,
Drifts of lovely leafy mould!

Grub the brambles, leave it clean;
Let no ivy-root be seen;
Elders, saplings all away,
Only the strong quicks may stay.
Pare the stubs to make them shoot,

155

Bend the headers to the root,
Drive the stakes, and strongly wind them,
With good hazel-suckers bind them.
Wait till June, then come and gloat;
You need not even shed your coat.
Whispering the keen hook glides
Over tender top and sides:
Then with calm unheated face,
Falling back a stately pace,
You will stand and view its grace.
Three feet high, and one foot through,
Neat and pretty, strong and new,
Your ancient tyrant kneels to you.

THE CYGNET

a Song of Thames

He sails alone, rocking on turbid water,
Water that has been fouled by wicked creatures:
Water whose loveliness dies of pollution,
The ermine water lapping royal London,
The ermine water that should match his whiteness,
Wafting him gaily over gleaming gravel;
But whose grey ripple to his cygnet dimness
Answers with broken images of sorrow.

For male pride, in the spring, he lifts his feathers,
Grey though they be; and thus with overarching
Pinions he goes, and lays his long neck backward,
Down-pointing the fierce narrow head and livid
Bill, that is now leaden, but shall be scarlet:
Vaunting himself, and moving like a haughty
Ship new returned from desperate adventures,
All the more terrible if she be tarnished.

But solitary he sails, moving unmated
Past the bright nuptial convoys, where the happy,
Blanched by the flux of time, scarlet and silver,
Breast the big tideway of the glorious river
To seek their beds among the secret marshes
And from their joy regenerate his passion:
Himself a mode of these, he passes hissing,
Dark in the face of love, mourning division.

Mourning division, in his ashy garment,
He the polluted element possesses
More than those pure, those all-completed lovers,
Who, their wide wandering for a time forsaken,
Go to the anchored nest among the rushes;
Of level solitude he takes dominion,
Also of the huge air, which they abandon;
That too, darkly defiled by wicked creatures:

Yet seen in the white morning as beautiful,
Dove-breasted smoky air over the dreadful
Gap-toothed black scribbled skylines such as madness
Might scrawl in dungeons; but for despair, unmeaning:
Over these evil visions the dove-breasted
Air, which they outrage, but which shall survive them,
Leans, as in transient tenderness the harlot
Forgets herself, thinking of her lost childhood.

In those dark places beauty is imprisoned;
Beauties, the confused remnants of broken races,
Bloom in brief pride, then sink away in squalor,
Die battling against the fall of filth unceasing,
Gap-toothed and blackened like the evil skyline,
Soiled and polluted; like the fair dove-breasted
Harlot the air, helpless against pollution:
Dreaming at times of happy love and childhood.

In that poor tender throng I see the flaxen
Heads, and I see the thin gleam gild the swarthy,
But the light centres on the high Milesian
Wonder, in whom the life like summer lightning
Played, and whose passion leaped abroad in flashes:
Clear as the keen new moon she glittered whitely,
With dark red hair, and eyes of the sea's colour.

She shall not pine, nor shall time's tedious poison
Tarnish the noble image newly minted,
Wear off the inscription: the gold piece is broken,
That avalanche of shards is heaped above her;
Rough pyramid enough for the rare beauty
Stamped by the mindless onslaught into fragments:
Mourn for the wine-red hair hidden for ever,
Mourn for sea-coloured eyes dismissed to darkness!

The fiery tears are falling; red and silver,
They change and drift and wane, stars of disaster;
Gold clusters, like the sparks in burning paper,
Silently glimmer, then from haunted darkness
Leaps their long shuddering voice of formal horror:
White sheets of light flicker and flap and vanish;
The steel-blue fingers, stark, intent and rigid,
Deliberately seek their prey in heaven.

The fiery rain is falling, and the vision
Of love is lost in the funereal blackness:
I heard a music once, but it is silent,
The bellowing night derides it and devours it
With loud destruction, varying but unceasing;
Where are the harp and the pipe now, my darling,
The loved voice murmuring in the leafy shadow?
All fallen silent, and all buried with thee.

The fiery doom is falling; fear and horror
Engulf me as the wave of steel roars over:
Shuddering with terror and the cold of winter,
Empty of life and yet impaled by duty,
I tremble as the dry stalks in a meadow
Tremble in barren wind, in stark December,
Sere, sere and barren as those bones of summer;
Where is my hope, O where lies any promise?

And loud within, life undefeated answers.
Even while the icy wind of terror rattles
In the dry brain, the thought comes quick upon me
Of seed blown from the skull-shaped pod and scattered,
Preparing a new beauty, an awakening;
So even in extremity the seed is with me,
Even in this utter night the bliss is latent,
Through mortal misery I bear the secret.

No statecraft, but the germ of hope undying
My seed is, key of the undiscovered kingdom;
Small winged seeds shaped like keys, scattered by terror,
Ejaculated from the skull in torment,
Torn from the bony husk and sown by fury
In strange far meadows and small secret places,
To flower in that immortal, promised summer,
When the sky weeps no fire, but only water.

Water shall bless them, water out of heaven
Washing from earth the stains of wicked creatures;
Soul of the ermine dying of pollution,
The martyred ermine dying and exhaling
Back the unmingled purity of water,
Absolving our corruption; incorrupted
Even though slain, exhaling into heaven
And redescending in continual pardon:

Water in rain, water in dew at evening
Falling through clear air, stealing through clean grasses,
Dwelling in darkness in our mother's body,
In secret springs welling and murmuring through her,
Gathering in brooks and lapsing into rivers,
Rolling magnificent down glorious tideways
Deep for the mighty hulls, clean for the salmon,
Pouring predestined to unfathomed ocean.

Restore our innocence, return with water
Bliss for the blood-guilt of the wicked creatures,
Whose life – like this noble polluted river
On which the sorry dawn now glimmers weakly,
And over which the smoke of late destruction
Scrawls the blear signature of madness – sickens
At the denial of its inmost nature,
Loathing its vileness, longing for its pardon.

The blear smoke crawls, the dawn glimmers, the children,
With their wan mothers, creep from dens that hide them
A little from their terror; they turn homeward
To the poor dole of food allotted strictly,
To each his portion, just and insufficient;
To the grey day; labouring on till evening,
Then turning blindly to the earth for harbour
As beasts do, bolting into holes in terror.

It is broad day; on the polluted river,
Thick with impurity yet crowned with honour,
There sails a creature raised above pollution,
Proud and immaculate as winter ermine,
He who was last year's Cygnet; now from greyness
Wholly redeemed; like the stream's peerless lily
He opens to the struggling sun his pinions,
Evoking from below the answering image.

Anger is past with him; the hissing madness
Of unrequited passion is forgotten:
See where she glides, and turns that look upon him
Which only death extinguishes once kindled;
For they like every noble thing are faithful,
Finding in love the only cure of sorrow,
Abandoning themselves each to the other,
Losing the separate self, the seed of anguish.

Go, vanish into the far secret places,
With the bright signature of love upon you;
Gathering in your breasts the sacred river
Of life, which through your royal blood flows onward,
Blooming in snow and fire, fulfilled for ever:
While we, still bound in anger and pollution,
Battle through dreary days and nights of terror
Until our spirit flowers, and we follow.

FREEMASONS OF THE AIR

It was enough to lie and stare
At these freemasons of the air,
The loved sandmartins, who had come
To scrape their cunning tunnelled home
In that else-wasted sandy bluff
We hoped was soft and tall enough:
To see the good-luck swallow sail
With turning wing and forky tail,
And highest in the diamond light
The swifts like boomerangs in flight,
The spirits who can sleep on high
And hold their marriage in the sky.

Sweetly they soar, and well agreed,
None quarrels with another's need:
Like deep-sea sailors from afar
Drawn home by their mysterious star,
They sport, they sing in unison,
Their noble perils make them one.

THE SWAN BATHING

Now to be clean he must abandon himself
To that fair yielding element whose lord he is.
There in the mid-current, where she is strongest:
Facing the stream, he half sinks, who knows how?
His armed head, his prow wave-worthy, he dips under:
The meeting streams glide rearward, fill the hollow
Of the proud wings: then as if fainting he falls sidelong,
Prone, without shame, reveals the shiplike belly
Tumbling reversed, with limp black paddles waving,
And down, gliding abandoned, helplessly wallows,
The head and neck, wrecked mast and pennon, trailing.

It is enough: satisfied he rears himself,
Sorts with swift movement his disordered tackle,
Rises, again the master; and so seated
Riding, with spreading wings he flogs the water
Lest she should triumph: in a storm of weeping
And a great rainbow of her tears transfigured,
With spreading circles of his force he smites her
Till remote tremblings heave her rushy verges
And all her lesser lives are rocked with rumour.

Now they are reconciled: with half-raised pinion
And backward-leaning head pensively sailing,
With silver furrow the reflected evening
Parting, he softly goes: and one cold feather
Drifts, and is taken gently by the rushes;
By him forgotten, and by her remembered.

162

THE SPARROW'S SKULL

Memento Mori. Written at the Fall of France.

The kingdoms fall in sequence, like the waves on the shore.
All save divine and desperate hopes go down, they are no more.
Solitary is our place, the castle in the sea,
And I muse on those I have loved, and on those who have loved me.

I gather up my loves, and keep them all warm,
While above our heads blows the bitter storm:
The blessed natural loves, of life-supporting flame,
And those whose name is Wonder, which have no other name.

The skull is in my hand, the minute cup of bone,
And I remember her, the tame, the loving one,
Who came in at the window, and seemed to have a mind
More towards sorrowful man than to those of her own kind.

She came for a long time, but at length she grew old;
And on her death-day she came, so feeble and so bold;
And all day, as if knowing what the day would bring,
She waited by the window, with her head beneath her wing.

And I will keep the skull, for in the hollow here
Lodged the minute brain that had outgrown a fear;
Transcended an old terror, and found a new love,
And entered a strange life, a world it was not of.

Even so, dread God! even so, my Lord!
The fire is at my feet, and at my breast the sword:
And I must gather up my soul, and clap my wings, and flee
Into the heart of terror, to find myself in thee.

VISION OF THE CUCKOO

Known by the ear; sweet voice, sour reputation;
Seen now and then at distance, the double bell
Dying along your flight; now secretly
From the small window darkened by the yew
I with the eye possess you and your meaning.

Secure you walk, picking your food under the roses.
The light on the large head is blue,
The wings are netted cinnamon and umber,
The soft dark eye is earthward, the silver belly
Gleams with reflected pink from fallen petals.

I by the world and by myself offended,
Bleeding with outraged love, burning with hate,
Embattled against time my conqueror
In mindbegotten, misbegotten space,
Drink with fierce thirst your drop of absolution.

No love, no hate, no self; only a life,
Blooming in timelessness, in unconceived
Space walking innocent and beautiful;
Guiltless, though myriad-life-devouring;
Guiltless, though tyrant to your fellow-fowls,
You live; and so in me one wound is healed,
Filled with a bright scar, coloured like the roses.

THE CROW

A bird, the master of the air,
Is flimsy, like a cheating toy.
It makes you sorry, if you care
For the loud song, the soaring joy,
For that taut hawk that looks so strong.
His bones are hollow, and his breast

164

Like a thin box of some frail wood.
Bad luck can never dog him long,
Soon comes the cold and the great rest.
Perhaps the creatures find it good.
Perhaps that kestrel, if it could
Speak with hooked beak, would say to me,
"So vulnerable joy must be."

I never held, living or dead,
The barred hawk in my grasping hand;
But once the children kept and fed
A crow they found in the meadow-land,
Whose foot was hurt, preventing him
From leaping up, and so from flight.
They thought that rest for his poor limb
In a small coop, would set him right.

And so it proved; but day by day,
Though more familiar and less lame,
He only lived to get away
And never, never could be tame:
Approach the shed in which he lay,
Up-wind, as softly as a cat;
Peep through the crack...his eye would say,
"You're there...I wonder what you're at?"

Taken in hand, he did not pant
And tremble, as the small birds do;
His gimcrack carcase gave no sign:
But his grim eye the postulant
To friendship damned with all he knew;
Each day he lost a little shine.

I knew a man, I knew a man
As thin as any grudging crow.
He also had his bitter *damn*
For all his jailers here below,
And also for the one above.
His hatred was a kind of faith;

And such a man one needs must love,
But does not mourn for at his death.

I loved him for his monstrous hate,
The blood-feud for the joy unborn,
Slain in the womb by gods and men:
I mourn him not, who know how great
His sin of separateness and scorn;
I wish he could be born again,
To think of hands as well as wings,
To walk the way of earthbound things;
Think less of getting, more of giving;
In short, to learn the art of living.

DUN-COLOUR

Subtle almost beyond thought are these dim colours,
The mixed, the all-including, the pervasive,
Earth's own delightful livery, banqueting
The eye with dimness that includes all brightness;
Complexity which the mind sorts out, as the sunlight
Resolves into many purities the mingled
Dun fleeces of the moorland; the quartz sparkles,
The rosy heath glows, the mineral-like mosses
And the heathbells and the myriad lichens
Start each into the eye a separate splendour:
So in the mind's sun bloom the dim dun-colours.

The dry vermilion glow of familiar redbreast
Is not his real glory: that is the greenish,
Light-toned, light-dissembling, eye-deceiving
Dun of his smooth-sloped back, and on his belly
The whitish dun is laid to deceive the shadow:
In the dear linnet the olive-dun is lovely,
And the primrose-duns in the yellowhammer: but most beguiling,
Perhaps because of the perfect shape, is the ash-dun,

That quietest, most urbane, unprofaneable colour
Reserved as her livery of beauty to the hedge-sparrow.
There is a royal azure in her blood,
As her eggs prove, and in her nature gold,
For her children's throats are kingcups; but she veils them,
Mingled and blended, in her rare dun-colour.

For the rose-duns, and the blue-duns, look to the finches:
For the clear clear brown-duns, to the fallow deer
(How the sudden tear smarts in the eye wearied of cities)
And for all these and more to the many toadstools,
Which alone have the violet-dun, livid yet lovely:
But the most delicate duns are seen in the gentle
Monkeys from the great forests, the silvan spirits:
Wonderful! that these, almost our brothers,
Should be dressed so rarely, in sulphurous-dun and greenish;
O that a man had grassy hair like these dryads!
O that I too were attired in such dun-colours!

WHAT IS THERE?

The delicate fox on soft and savage feet
Comes to the cave in the place that is very high;
High and lonely and cold, where the winds meet;
And he glances in with a sidelong and savage eye;
The wind ruffles the silk of his savage hair,
As he glances within, and sees but a possible lair:

But this is the cave of crystal, the beautiful place,
Where from the morning of time the cold and severe
Colourless prisms of truth have grown from the face
Of the inchoate rock, and the Law is here;
But food and shelter are lords of the savage eye,
Blind to the affirmation of symmetry.

And in the cold mountain the ptarmigan couches in snow,
White upon white in the wild of the high Himalay,
Where through the whiteness the rosy primulas grow,
Banners of love in the stony dazzle of day:
But he hugs the snow and hollows it with his breast,
And sees not the glory glancing over his crest.

Lord, father, mother, and love! such is the sin
Of us all, such the sin of the savage eye,
That we see but a lair whenever we look within
The temple; we see not the banner of love borne by:
Only, (packed in the snowdrift, couched in the lair)
One rears a savage head and questions the air;
One among millions, dimly, asks what is there.

HOVERFLY ON POPPY

Like a man reaping, on the mealy edge
Of the blond Poppy's anther-ring he stands,
Pressing his breast against the fecund hedge,
And gathering the pollen as with hands;
Glittering heroic on the gold and red
He ravishes his bright Lethean bread.

So, licensed by a large fertility,
The robber and the robbed stand close embraced;
Curtailing hopes of generation, he
But steals some love from what has love to waste,
And gives it a strange nursling: that which flies,
Darts like a death, and looks with myriad eyes.

THE SMALL PLANT

I must die! O was I born
For time's malice and man's scorn?

Look, where at your feet the Plant,
Love's pilgrim and poor suppliant,
With a leaf like a small hand
Signals to you from the sand;
With a flower like a blue eye
Propounds love's dreadful mystery;
With a weak triumphant spire
Soars to a peak of pure desire.
So poor, so circumscribed she stands,
Foot-fast; and yet her little hands
Sweep in spirals, and describe
The old pattern of her tribe,
Her awful rune, the which she must
Repeat ere she return to dust,
Completing with a meagre seed
The implacable and humble need,
The spell, the prayer, the proud pavane,
Conceived before those hills began.

ONE TREE TO THE NORTH

We need no grove; one yew-tree to the north suffices
Against the snow and the rain, the wind and the hail:
The old roof, weak and botched with mean devices,
Is still unpierced by stealth of water, unstripped by gale:
The little tottering window in the north-east gable
Would have been gone, but for the tree, these hundred years;
But we can still turn the thin old latch, graceful and feeble,
And look through the thronging red branches where each one bears
Thousands of wiry twigs, and a night of leaves
(Narrow and neat and dark, like some kinds of faith);

169

A bulwark of trapped air to the crumbling eaves,
A shield against time, against change, and against death.

O stand still, and look long, and hold yourself quiet,
For there is the blessed throstle sunning his breast,
Finding a house, and a singing-place, and part of his diet
In those galleries of the tree that look to the east.
Nothing that can be seen or sung is fairer
Than the waxen seed whose cup is green and then red,
Ripening as the faintheart elms grow barer,
And hanging over the blessed throstle's head.

O my dark tree, my one tree to the north,
Coming to me out of the north and out of the past,
Guardian alike of the sleepers in bed and in earth
Against the demons of middle air and the blast –
The blast of storm, or the blast of the thousand-pounder –
Stand with us a little longer, still stand fast
Until the venerable roof falls and the walls founder,
And flourish over the ruined hearth at the last.

THE TALL FRUIT-TREES

I'll lop them, it will be easier so to tend them;
    Then we may clean them, and gather the fruit with ease;
    No one can do with these great old orchard trees,
Dirty, shady, unwieldy – don't try to defend them.

O promise to do them one or two at a time then –
    That will make you twenty years in going the rounds:
Then the tall tops for me will be out of bounds,
    Surely I shall no longer be able to climb then.

But while I am able O let me ascend the plum-tree
    And poke my head out at the top, where the lovely view
Has a foreground of scarlet plums with a wash of blue,
    And I am away from earth in the starlings' country.

And for a few years yet spend a day in the pear-tree,
    Squirming and stretching, plagued by the wasps and the twigs,
Scratches all over me, bruised in the arms and legs,
    Coming down whacked at last from the great old bare tree –

And yet not wholly bare, for his topmost steeple
    Still flaunts a fair wreath of a dozen, the best of all;
Ha, he beat me at last, for he was so tall –
    He will not give his best work up to greedy people.

And there is the huge gaunt apple-tree, dead man's seedling,
    With five great limbs, spreading twenty feet from the ground;
How he makes us stagger the longest ladder around,
    So heavy – yet four feet short of the ladder we're needing.

Some years he's good for bushels of small red apples
    That keep well enough, and roast well enough by the fire,
But every year he is young and brave with desire,
    Smothered in rosy wreaths that the sunlight dapples.

Dappled with sunlight and bright with the May-time raindrop,
    Mighty from age and youthful with tender bloom,
He heaves up brightness and scent to our highest room,
    Brushes the dormer-window with shining maintop.

We'll take in a bit more ground, and plant it with limber
    Maidens on dwarfing stocks, at twelve feet apart;
But the great old trees are the real loves of my heart,
    Mountains of blossom and fruit on the stalwart timber.

THE BAT

Lightless, unholy, eldritch thing,
Whose murky and erratic wing
Swoops so sickeningly, and whose
Aspect to the female Muse
Is a demon's, made of stuff
Like tattered, sooty waterproof,
Looking dirty, clammy, cold.

Wicked, poisonous, and old:
I have maligned thee!... for the Cat
Lately caught a little bat,
Seized it softly, bore it in.
On the carpet, dark as sin
In the lamplight, painfully
It limped about, and could not fly.

Even fear must yield to love,
And pity makes the depths to move.
Though sick with horror, I must stoop,
Grasp it gently, take it up,
And carry it, and place it where
It could resume the twilight air.

Strange revelation! warm as milk,
Clean as a flower, smooth as silk!
O what a piteous face appears,
What great fine thin translucent ears!
What chestnut down and crapy wings,
Finer than any lady's things –
And O a little one that clings!

Warm, clean, and lovely, though not fair,
And burdened with a mother's care:
Go hunt the hurtful fly, and bear
My blessing to your kind in air.

AGED CUPID

The old man with the washed cord breeks,
The man who cuts the hedge so clean,
The little man with rosy cheeks,
The man whose merry eyes have been
Never more bright, if far more keen;
The man who keeps the bonfire in,
Keeps the great heap through days and weeks
Smouldering in secret, slow and sure;
Who chops a sapling with his bill
Down in a trice – the sly demure
Old laughing man who sits so still,
Subtly achieving all his will,
Who having tools cannot be poor:

Who turns the least mishap to mirth,
Shrieking at withered cucumbers,
And doubled up because of dearth
In what his grim old girl calls hers –
The lagging parsley-bed, or fine
Sweet-peas gone droughty, bristling sere
Where last week saw a brilliant line;
Or seedling beets one morning here,
The next day eaten by the flea –
Convulsive spleen to you and me,
But one more heaven-sent joke to he:

The women's favourite, pretty lad,
And pretty still at seventy-four,
He'd like to go upon the gad,
To make the lasses laughing-mad,
As he has often done before;
To make them dance to violin
Or the heart-wiling concertina
Till legs grow weak and breath comes thin
And even the fattest wench is leaner:
Till the mad settle dances too,
And dust befogs the whirling mazes,

173

And the choked lamp-wick splutters blue,
And beer and money go like blazes –

What is he up to now? Go see;
Creep on the grass without a sound.
So rapt and so intent is he
He's brewing some young devilry –
Good Lord! look what the man has found!
A well-grown Viper, which he nips
Behind the head, and with a fork
Of the bat-willow's limber tips
Pins to the earth – what devil's work!
It is for his staid son to find.
At evening when he weeding goes,
Under the dewy favourite Rose
The furious serpent will be twined:
He'll howl with horror first, then see
The artifice, and bawl with rage,
While the old rogue, I will engage,
Will almost weep for ecstasy:
Come, girls, and tell me, who is he?

ON AN OLD POEM

Like the small soft unchanging flower
      The words in silence speak;
Obedient to their ancient power
      The tear stands on my cheek.

Though our world burn, the small dim words
      Stand here in steadfast grace,
And sing, like the indifferent birds
      About a ruined place.

Though the tower fall, the day be done,
  The night be drawing near,
Yet still the tearless tune pipes on,
  And still evokes the tear:

The tearless tune, wiser than we,
  As weak and strong as grass,
Or the wild bracken-fern we see
  Spring where the palace was.

THE COLOURED GLASS

To M.E.A.

To the opaque, hostile, insoluble
World, I hold up, as children the coloured glass,
My sundry specula; the thin leaves
As blood-dissembling emeralds; against death
The one-day flower; to exorcize unlove
The loved much-loving face.

Where the mind fails the miracle translates,
Makes plain the equivocating oracle;
With seed at least, where bloom
Fades, parries winter: answers with a kiss
The crack of doom, and to the bending mast
Nails the bright flag that else were glad to fall.

RETROSPECT

A sylvan place, a distant time,
An owlish and an elvish air,
The evening, and the autumn rime,
And the rapt creature roaming there

I see; and though I know return
Is not, and would not have it so,
There is a thing that I would learn,
There is a secret I would know,

Which that could tell, if it were kind,
Which wanders the remembered land
With shreds of legend in its mind
And a few berries in its hand.

It looks upon the ragged tree,
It broods along the darkening glade;
It sees what I no longer see,
Glories and yearns and is afraid

At something in the smouldering sky,
At something in the tangled thorn:
In universal mystery
It walks enchanted and forlorn.

The cloud, the stone, the trembling plant
Address it in their silent tongue:
The treasure of the ignorant,
The magic of the hapless young,

Brim its full soul, and though too weak
The incantation to express,
For cloud and stone and leaf to speak
To justify its idleness,

It sees what I no longer see,
It hears what is to me unheard:
If it could only speak to me,
Shaping the wonder to a word,

If it could speak the ancient spell,
Then I could dress it in a rhyme,
And tune it like the village bell,
Heard down the darkening glade of time.

O would it speak, and would it stay,
And would it try to understand;
Or smile aside, and turn away
With the small berries in its hand?

BETTER THAN LOVE

Are you there? Can you hear?
Listen, try to understand.
O be still, become an ear,
For there is darkness on this land.
Stand and hearken, still as stone,
For I call to you alone.

Who can be what the weed was
In the empty afternoon?
Who can match me the wild grass,
Sighing its forgotten tune:
Who is equal to that shell,
Whose spiral is my parable?

No human eye reflects the weed
Burning beneath the lonely sun:
The wild hard grass spangled with seed
Is still unmatched by anyone:
The justice of the shell is still
Above the mind, above the will.

Since love and beauty, blown upon,
Are not desired, nor spoken of,
Hear me, you solitary one,
Better than beauty or than love,
Seen in the weed, the shell, the grass,
But never in my kind, alas!

The ragged weed is truth to me,
The poor grass honour, and the shell
Eternal justice, till I see
The spirit rive the roof of hell
With light enough to let me read
More than the grass, the shell, the weed.

THE LOST TRIBE

How long, how long must I regret?
I never found my people yet;
I go about, but cannot find
The blood-relations of the mind.

Through my little sphere I range,
And though I wither do not change;
Must not change a jot, lest they
Should not know me on my way.

Sometimes I think when I am dead
They will come about my bed,
For my people well do know
When to come and when to go.

I know not why I am alone,
Nor where my wandering tribe is gone,
But be they few, or be they far,
Would I were where my people are!

RAINY SUMMER

Remember, though we cannot write it, the delicate dream.
Though the wheat be cankered, the woodbine and wild rose
Drink, and exhale in perfume their pensive being:
The lily's life prolonged plays on to an extreme
And elegiac poignancy; the bee goes
Solitary with subdued hum in the green, beyond our seeing.

We are spirits, though, the dream denied, we are also ghosts.
We repose in our secret place, in the rainy air,
By the small fire, the dim window, in the ancient house;
Kind to the past, and thoughtful of our hosts,
Shadows of those now beyond thought and care,
Phantoms that the silence engenders, the flames arouse.

Those we have never seen, and those we shall see no more,
Haunting the tender gloom and the wan light,
Are there, as the secret bird is there, is betrayed
By the leaf that moved when she slipped from her twig by the door,
As the mouse unseen is perceived by her gliding shade,
As the silent owl is known by the wind of her flight.

Thus poor, forgotten, in a summer without sun,
In a decaying house, an unvisited place,
We remember the delicate dream, the voice of the clay;
Recalling the body before the life was begun,
Stealing through blood and bone with bodiless grace
In the elfish night and green cool gloom of the day.

THE SERIOUS CHILD

O which is more, the pleasure or the pain,
    To see the child who knows
At nine years old, the tale of loss and gain,
    The weight of the world's woes:

179

Joy for the sacrificial love he learns,
	Or grief for light heart lost?
See, in some farthing matter, how he yearns,
	And sighs, and counts the cost!

He feels his weakness, sees the weary road
	That others go, and he,
On slender shoulders taking up his load
	Fares forth as mournfully.

Child, are we lost? and shall we ever find
	The far abode of joy?
Only within, in kingdoms of the mind,
	My little careworn boy.

DEATH OF A BEAUTY

What is it tears at the vitals, why does the eye
Gush over with sudden violence, like a broken dam?
The containing mind dissolve with a shameless cry
At the mere printed conjunction, death with a name?
This is the power of beauty which none denies,
The spell of visual harmony, which when we see
All are enamoured, living only in the eyes,
Asking no more than sight of the mystery –
To see the thing stated, though unsolved, unpossessed.
Praying as if to the perfect orb of the sun
That gives life, but in whose bosom no life may rest,
So do we gaze upon the beautiful one:
And now that sun has gone down, that day is done.

We will cover our heads for a time and weep our fill.
For a short time will be dissolved in woe,
Since the heroic limbs are stiff and still,
And that face is gone where all the faces go;
As when the flowers and the fair leaves depart,
Leaving but winter in the weary land,

180

And a worse winter in the weary heart,
An ill-clad back, and nothing in the hand.

The beautiful live as it were in a waking sleep.
Lulled in the trance of harmony, they do not know
How we are wounded and famished, wallowing deep
In that black misery and bitter flow
They are exempt from: yet looking in their eyes
We worship, and not envy: to us it seems
There is our discord resolved, and our miseries
Balmed in a sovereign slumber and healed in dreams.
We will empty ourselves of tears, and it will be over.
For them we do not harbour abiding pain.
Long pain is all for our own, the friend or the lover
Who bleeds by our side, like us who bows to the rain.
The tempest of tears for the broken vessel of crystal,
For the symbolic face, for death and a name;
For the impersonal, the bright-clad vestal,
The fallen rose of the world, not the slain lamb.

LILIES AND WINE

The white and gold flowers and the wine,
Symbols of all that is not mine,
Stand sacramental, and so bless
The wounded mind with loveliness
That it leaps blindly to evade
The world's anguish there portrayed.
What of the water and the green?
I know what leaves and water mean –
The bright blade and the limpid flow,
I knew and loved them long ago;
But now the white, the gold, the blood
Dawn doomlike, not to be withstood.

At the white, gold, and crimson gate
I and my heart stand still and wait.

BUT FOR LUST

But for lust we could be friends,
    On each other's necks could weep:
In each other's arms could sleep
    In the calm the cradle lends:

Lends awhile, and takes away.
    But for hunger, but for fear,
Calm could be our day and year
    From the yellow to the grey:

From the gold to the grey hair,
    But for passion we could rest,
But for passion we could feast
    On compassion everywhere.

Even in this night I know
    By the awful living dead,
By this craving tear I shed,
    Somewhere, somewhere it is so.

THE HILL OF THE KINDRED

To K. O'H.

Would you remember if I asked you
The ruin in the hanging wood?
The close grove and the hill had tasked you –
There in the gloom we paused and stood:
In the green gloom the tumbled stones,
The cold black gaping chimney-place,
Showed like a heap of sorry bones,
Like a skull's face for a man's face;
A bitter sight for youth! We sighed,
Seeing (we thought) oppressive years

Coming with slow funereal stride,
And one among them with the Shears.
But now a ruin is to me
A place of peace, where restless care,
Parting, and toil, and usury,
And all our sorrows buried are;
I think how she who baked the bread
On this poor hearth when it was warm
Sleeps like a queen among the dead
With her last trouble in her arm:
And though her elder brood abound
And flourish, and have got them land
In many a fertile valley round,
Here rather on the hill I stand
In memory, and lay my head
Down on the green neglected stone,
Loving the cold hearth of the dead
And the wild weed that lives alone:
Not timid, like an untried child,
Nor bitter, like an angry lover;
For life and I are reconciled,
The grief is done, the care is over.

WILD HONEY

You, the man going along the road alone,
Careless or wretched, rarely thoughtful, never serene,
Possessing nothing worth having; man of the sickly pleasures,
Man of the mawkish, wrong-headed sorrows, typical man:

The wealth is there, man of the empty pocket,
The gold is there, man of the greying hair,
And the sweetness, man whose life is bitter as ashes,
The good work, the accomplished work, the wonderful artifice,
The wonderful artefact, man of the useless hands.

There in the riddled tree, hanging in darkness,
There in the roof of the house and the wall-hollow,
The new like pearl, the old like magical amber,
Hidden with cunning, guarded by fiery thousands
(See where they stream like smoke from the hole in the gable),
There in the bank of the brook the immortal secret,
In the ground under your feet the treasure of nations,
Under the weary foot of the fool, the wild honey.

"POLYMORPH PERVERS"

At the blind end of the house,
Where the weeping stains of rain come creeping down,
Where the forlorn winds arouse
Once again the withered leaf and brown,
And harry it and hunt it up and down;
In that place where no one goes,
Sudden joy, the shooting star,
Rootless joy burst out like the wild rose,
Shattering sorrow, breaking winter's bar;
Furious joy leaped up in me,
Where little joy or none might be.

By the clean, the fruitful tree,
Where the bright leaf shades the big plums flushed with fire,
Where the searching eye can see
Through the harvest, buds of young desire,
The next wave of the tides that never tire;
In the presence of the blessing, the pure woe,
Breaking like a winter wave,
Filled the hollow bosom with its flow;
Filled it like some sandy, sterile cave
With wreck, and weed, and agony,
The lendings of the bitter sea.

LAMENT FOR ONE'S SELF

I know best what moan to make
Over my own dead;
Grieving aloud for my own sake,
Muttering at my grave's head.

Did you get what you wanted,
Fine child as you were?
I was harried and hunted
Till I took refuge here.

Did you see the fine sights
With your good clear eyes?
Foul sights and strange delights
Till blear age hid the skies.

My strong teeth that were so white
All went to decay;
My muscles and my clear sight
Wasted away.

Did you find the true heart
For whom you were born?
Never, for cold lust did part
Us in this place forlorn.

It is either that we all are mad,
Or my heart was born blind,
For every kind of love went bad
Between me and my kind.

Did you see nothing that could seem
Perfect, as life should be?
Yes; for the birds were like my dream,
And the leaves on the tree:

And the dear stainless buds of spring,
When upward they did move;
And many another gentle thing
Seemed fit for life and love.

And here and there someone would play,
Or make so fine a song
That all my sorrow fled away,
And there was nothing wrong.

But in the life the people led,
With sorrow day and night,
Vast wars, babes slaughtered, wicked bread —
O there was nothing right.

Then do you hate your being,
Curse the day you were born?
No, for another seeing
Makes me not all forlorn.

No matter what the body felt,
No matter what it saw,
My inmost spirit ever knelt
In a blind love and awe:

And dead or living knows full well,
Sick or whole it knows,
The secret it may never tell
Of joy and of repose.

PASSION AND PEACE

Poetry, like all passion, seeks for peace.
Wild creature, look into the pool and learn.
There in the level water shines the face,
The summer eyes that can both weep and burn,
Mirrored so calmly in the quiet place;
Fire in sweet water lulled, questions that turn
At long last to the simple need for rest.
Have I not still the peace of the unborn,
Have I not learned of death to be possessed?
O put off passion, and with passion scorn,
And think that this quiet water is my breast,
Calm, yet without that image, most forlorn.
O let the fervour of the princely sun,
Which makes the desert solitary, sleep
Here in the water his dominions weep,
Binding all peace and passion into one.

FLOWERS IN THE FACTORY

The firedew, the glow-worm light,
Phosphor-radiance, molten heart,
Make a clearness in the night;
Lend these poor a little part
Of the beauty of the sun!
None can tell who does not know
How such stars in beauty run
With cold sweetness like the snow
Through the silent, suffering mind,
Through the grime and through the gloom
Like the fair, the fleeing hind
Through the forest to her doom,
Followed till she vanishes
By beauty-tranced, by yearning eyes.

187

Give them blossoms, what you can.
What is nature in your hand
Changes in this mood of man.
You will never understand
How your fair familiar Rose
With her soon-expiring breath
Like a loving martyr goes
To comfort wretches by her death;
How the Jonquil's tender face,
Like a spirit sent to save,
Like a love discovered in a dreadful place,
Lights a candle in the cruel grave.

FUNERAL WREATHS

In the black bitter drizzle, in rain and dirt,
The wreaths are stacked in the factory entrance-yard.
People gather about them. Nobody's hurt
At the rank allusion to death. Down on the hard
Cobblestones go the painted girls on their knees
To read what the football-club has put on the card.
There is interest, and delight, and a sense of ease.
Is it only that flowers smell sweet, and are pretty and bright,
Or because of the senseless waste of so many pounds,
Or because in that dreadful place the unwonted sight
Of a heap of blossom is balm to unconscious wounds –
The mortal wounds that benumb, not the sharp raw pains
Of the daily misery, but the fatal bleeding inside?
Here is the supernatural to be bought with the gains
Of the spectral torment. The soul can go for a ride
On the high-heaped car that has nothing to do with bread,
Nothing, nothing at all to do with the war;
The soul can go for a ride with the rich young dead.
It makes you feel like a wedding. The Gates Ajar,
The Broken Column, the Pillow with "Rest in Peace,"
The sham Harp with its tinsel string allusively bust,

The three-quid Cross made of flaring anemones,
The gibbetted carnations with steel wires thrust
Right through their rankling midriffs, the skewered roses,
Tulips turned inside-out for a bolder show,
Arum lilies stuck upright in tortured poses
Like little lavatory-basins – these victims grow
In a private garden for each, in a heavenly soil.
Mindless and pagan offering, wicked waste,
This is the efflorescence of godless toil,
Something that has no meaning, that has no taste,
Something that has no use but to cry aloud,
Going up to the gates of life with a formless din,
"We are the lost, betrayed ones. We are the Crowd.
Think, for you must do something to let us in."

SINKING

O I am spent, I have no more strength to swim.
The blessed sun touches the bitter sea's rim:
I cannot see the headland or the little town,
All my limbs are weary, and I must go down.

O is it sleep or love or death I most need,
And what peace shall I find in the arms of the weed?
The gulf-weed shall take me and cradle me in brown
Wide-waving tresses, for I must go down.

Go down under the sweet, the bitter flow:
You are the blind, but the blessed spirits know
Whether in sleep, or love, or death you must drown;
Cease then your striving, sink and go down.

SEABORN

Is there peace, is there peace
On any shore or shoal of these
Flowing seas, ebbing seas,
The dim deeps or the estuaries,
Or in that tide-resounding cave
Filled by the unwearying, weary wave?
Shall that deity ever set
Her breast veined like the violet
And her slender, her still hand
By that wave, on that sand;
Sleeping like a lovely doe
Where so late the bitter flow
Beat the shore and vexed it so?

Yes, be sure that she shall lie
Your loud shores and beaches by;
With a sweet blind look shall come
To strike all the roaring dumb,
With a small and sleeping face
To spread stillness in that place
Where the enemies embrace.

What is she, what is she,
This wonder that shall come to me?
When on the sea-sand she lies
With sleeping face and hidden eyes,
Shall I know her lovely name,
Or the place from whence she came,
Or her meaning? Having kept
Faithful silence while she slept,
Shall I see her waking eyes
Making clear the mysteries
Which before I searched in vain;
And shall the sweet and subtle rain
Bless the salty shores that were
Barren, wild, and beaten bare,
And make the fine grass flourish there?

Gentle peace, blessed peace,
She shall calm your raging seas,
Every shore and shoal of these;
Subtle rain shall stay their want,
Bringing life where life was scant,
By the dry shell, the tender plant:
Faithful silence earn the sight
Of those fair eyes' unknown delight;
And the mystery that dwells
In the deep gulf, in the dry shells,
In the bare and beaten stone
Which the brine still streams upon,
Shall dissolve in calm, and yield
To that old light new revealed
Their true being, and a sense
As of ultimate innocence
Born of pain, and only found
On such long-tormented ground,
There where the unresting seas
Fashion the perfect pearl of peace.

See her laid in the cave's light
As waveworn alabaster white,
With faint mouth on which are set
The rose-hue and fragrance yet,
And breast like the white violet:
With one still and slender hand
On the sea-forsaken sand,
And one hand beneath the face
That makes brightness in the place
Where the enemies embrace.

THE ESTUARY

Light, stillness and peace lie on the broad sands,
On the salt-marshes the sleep of the afternoon.
The sky's immaculate; the horizon stands
Steadfast, level and clear over the dune.

There are voices of children, musical and thin,
Not far, nor near, there in the sandy hills;
As the light begins to wane, so the tide comes in,
The shallow creek at our feet silently fills:

And silently, like sleep to the weary mind,
Silently, like the evening after the day,
The big ship bears inshore with the inshore wind,
Changes her course, and comes on up through the bay,

Rolling along the fair deep channel she knows,
Surging along, right on top of the tide.
I see the flowery wreath of foam at the bows,
The long bright wash streaming away from her side:

I see the flashing gulls that follow her in,
Screaming and tumbling, like children wildly at play,
The sea-born crescent arising, pallid and thin,
The flat safe twilight shore shelving away.

Whether remembered or dreamed, read of or told,
So it has dwelt with me, so it shall dwell with me ever:
The brave ship coming home like a lamb to the fold,
Home with the tide into the mighty river.

QUORUM PORUM[1]

In a dark garden, by a dreadful tree,
The Druid Toms were met. They numbered three,
Tab Tiger, Demon Black, and Ginger Hate.
Their forms were tense, their eyes were full of fate;
Save the involuntary caudal thrill,
The horror was that they should sit so still.
An hour of ritual silence passed: then low
And marrow-freezing, Ginger moaned "OROW",
Two horrid syllables of hellish lore,
Followed by deeper silence than before.
Another hour, the tabby's turn is come;
Rigid, he rapidly howls "MUM MUM MUM";
Then reassumes his silence like a pall,
Clothed in negation, a dumb oracle.
At the third hour, the black gasps out "AH BLURK!"
Like a lost soul that founders in the murk;
And the grim, ghastly, damned and direful crew
Resumes its voiceless vigilance anew.
The fourth hour passes. Suddenly all three
Chant "WEGGY WEGGY WEGGY" mournfully,
Then stiffly rise, and melt into the shade,
Their Sabbath over, and their demons laid.

[1] *Porum:* Genitive plural of "Puss".

THE TALKING FAMILY

With the early morning tea
  Start the day's debates.
Soon the Talking Family
  Gathers, gravitates
To the largest room and bed,
That all may share in what is said.

193

All the Cats forgather too,
  With a calm delight,
Tab and ginger, long-haired blue,
  Seem to think it right
That they should share to some extent
In this early parliament.

Perhaps they only want a drink
  (Which of course they get)
But myself I like to think
  That the Cats are met
Because this animal rejoices
In the sound of human voices.

What they are we do not know,
  Nor what they may become.
Perhaps the thoughts that ebb and flow
  In a human home
May blow to brightness the small spark
They carry through the vasty dark.[1]

[1] Perque pruinosas tulit *irrequieta* tenebras. – OVID.

MISTER THE BLITZKIT

For K.

Double, double, toil and trouble,
Crumps and bumps and lumps of rubble.
Little Mister, six weeks old,
Hungry, frightened, dirty, cold,
Has no mother, home, nor dinner,
But he's sharp for a beginner.
From his crevice he surveys
Those who walk the ruined ways;
From their faces he can tell

194

Who would treat a kitten well.
The big policeman, good but gruff –
Let him pass; he's rather rough,
And as a conscientious man
Might pop him in a certain Van.
A kindly matron comes to view.
She's nice – but what about the stew?
When her four fat kids have done
There's not much left for anyone.
Besides, those kids would give him hell.
Let her go, then. Wait a spell.
Here's a warden; that's a frost –
He's got no home except his post.
Soldier, sailor – damn, no good.
Cripes, he could down a bit of food.
And O hell, here comes the rain.
Stick it, Mister, try again.

Ah, here she comes, the very one!
The fact is obvious as the sun.
Young as he is, now Mister knows
He can bid farewell to woes.
In her countenance he reads
That she will satisfy his needs.
Food, fire, bed – he ticks them off –
Worm-dose, mixture for his cough,
Velvet mouse for when he plays,
Brush and comb, and holidays
In the countryside afar,
Or boarded out with loving char.
She will pick him up correctly
And always touch him circumspectly,
Like a really first-class mother
Never neglect, yet never bother.
The greatest wonder is that he
Knows that there is a vacancy,
Which has allowed a thieving band
Of mice to get the upper hand.

Forth he darts – with piteous grace
Looks up mewing in her face.
Six weeks old – but what a grip
On the art of salesmanship!
Youth, dirt, fear, all play their part
In the lady's feeling heart.
A word of love, a mutual kiss,
And he is hers, and she is his.
Because he is so small and weak
She holds him closely to her cheek,
Takes him home, through wind and rain,
And will not let him go again.

Arrived, he finds he did not err
In his estimate of her.
Warm milk, a nice old woollen vest,
And he soon sinks to blissful rest.
When he awakes, his coat will be
Brushed into strict propriety,
And in the evening she will seal
Their love with a substantial meal,
And let him lay his clever head
Close to her own warm heart, in bed.

THE NEUTER-CAT'S APOTHEOSIS

Aged, thin-legged, tabby-and-white, and wise,
Poor Plainey held his tongue, and used his eyes.
Full seventeen years a hunter's life he led,
With seldom better food than broth and bread,
The heartless mess that rural England pours
On dirty plates for faithful carnivores.
And what with this, and his declining years,
He showed thin fur, stiff joints, and cankered ears.
Yet neither ageing limbs nor shabby coat
Hampered his prowess when he KILLED THE STOAT;

Yea, perched on water-butt, aloft, unseen,
Dropped in the nick, and nipped, and killed him clean.
This, and his lesser triumphs of the chase,
Assured him, while he lived, a certain place,
Yet, as a mere yard-cat, he had his share
Of want, and cold, and wretchedness to bear.
Demotic Venus, in the tabby she,
Never had any sort of use for he:
Insultingly aware he was no suitor,
She cuffed his chops because he was a neuter,
Or, coming on him where he sunning sat,
She with true female venom loudly spat.
The eunuch's chief delight, his daily food,
Still disappointed, for it was not good.
Of eave-scooped nestlings he could sometimes pull
In spring, a few, but not a bellyful;
And to eat rats and such he was too nice,
For rodentophagy's a feline vice;
While as for sleep, the other neutral boon,
Summer, that comes too late and goes too soon,
Afforded some snug naps in loft or skip,
But winter meant the cart-shed and its drip.

Heaven had decreed thee, Plainey, in thine age,
Some little recompense for life so sage.
A neighbouring house, where vile smallholder dwelt
(So far from wisely, that the purlieus smelt),
The churl, whom bad times thwacked for want of sense,
Sold for a song, and whining shambled thence;
And Kick-cat Hall, where Plainey dared not show
His clay-hued nose for fear of sudden blow,
And where conditions gave his nerves the jitters,
Became (O happy day) a nest of Pitters.
These kindly people served a charming god
Whose creed associated Cats with Cod;
Who put into their heads, when fowls they had,
That Giblets make the feline bosom glad;
And also, when there is not much to do,
That Pads and Ears sometimes need looking to.

197

Puss in their kitchen munched the proteid scrap,
Or even, elevated to a lap,
Suffered the dubious boon he could not quite
Relish, and did his best to seem polite.
He spruced himself, his ears were not so sore;
He licked his white feet at the kindly door,
Nor dreamed that heaven intended something more.

One Christmas season, from her lair in town,
The Author condescendingly came down
To spend a country Christmas, and to eat
Turkey, the which she does not deem a treat,
But half despises, and would liefer see
An honest Goose, or Beef for jollity.
Comes Boxing-day, and in the kitchen stands
The snooty bard, and hacks with vengeful hands
At the huge avian corpse, whose thirty pound
She thinks would have been better underground.
Old Plainey at the door his knowing lugs
Twitches, and opes and shuts his feeling pugs,
While from white-currant eyes much eloquence
He pours against the poet's subtle sense.
When of philosophy folk have a smattering
A philosophic confidence is flattering.
Plainey, whose life is spent in taking notes,
Can deal with female bards as well as stoats;
Mews to the Muse, and claims community
For Barn and Grub-Street in life's tragedy.
"Hard times," he says, "have taught me discipline;
I ask no more than some odd piece of skin;
The tears of things as poet you perceive –
Of you I ask, your wisdom gives me leave."
So mannerly, so sadly does he beg,
She from the turkey rends a mighty leg,
And with a royal gesture holds the limb
(Some twenty tough dry ounces) down to him,
Or nearly so – for sudden Plainey leapt,
And seized the trophy like a true adept;
And who shall say whether his clutching claws

First touched it, or his well-instructed jaws?
One moment, with the hunter's cunning old,
He stayed to jerk it to a better hold:
The next, like skimming Monoplane was seen
(With turkey-leg for wings) to scour the green,
His dearest object – nay, his only care –
To gain with speed his subterwoodpile lair,
And in the secret cave he wotted of
To express a neuter lifetime's frustrate love:
To have enough; in short, to get outside
The miracle that life had not denied.

Far through the backward era murky
Methinks I see that home-grown turkey!
To think that I could once despise
A tender bird of such a size!
Ah Plainey, in the rearward view
How I do sympathise with you:
How humbly do I hope to see
Another Turkey such as he,
With spreading breast, and fallen-hero legs,
Enough for any Cat or Bard that begs.

MUSA TRANSLATED

(With apologies to William Blake)

There Musa inhabited with horror – there
With River-Foggs and Murkiness and Smuts continual,
Under the unending Downpour of Stygian Coaldust
From Lot's-Road, where if Mrs Lot had been so silly
As to have turn'd into Salt, she would have been blackt-out
In a Night and a Day: where the dismall Fume ariseth
From the Place where they will not stop making the hellish Crucibles;
Where Housewives decline the Attempt to keep clean any more,
For (as they mournfully affirm) it's no use busting yourself,

When you've got round the Place once, it's time to start cleaning again.
And this Place, by the tortuousness of the Human Genius,
Costs dearly, and is accounted a desirable Neighbourhood.
There liv'd the Cat Musa, enwrapt in her Female Garment,
And there she conceiv'd her Young amid demon sexual Howlings
Appropriate to those Bohemian Haunts – far different from the gentle
Regenerated Accents, the heavenly Voice of Sublimated Love.
But when to the Charms of the Blessed Region were added
The squalling Alert and the sickening Scream and Whump
Of sacrilegious Projectiles, scathing th' idyllic Cradle
Of so many and various Loves – when Beings with tin Hats
And too many Whiskers stood on the Edges of Craters
Trying to recall if that were the Place where they had once liv'd with
    a Model
For almost three Weeks, and kindly hoping that the Fair One
(If that were the place indeed) had been luckily evicted
For non-payment of Rent, before the hellish Catastrophe –
Then indeed did the Owners of Musa, a worthy Couple
Of the stockbroking Sort, who affected our murky Strand
Out of pure Snobbishness, and Meekness to grown-up Children –
Think of their Cottage in Essex with modest Satisfaction.
And seeing that the fair Musa was great with Young
They popt her into the Car, enclosed in a Basket.
She, vibrant with Rage and Fear, imperative protesting,
Hurling herself with hysterick Leaps against the Enclosure,
Cursing the Universe in general, and more particularly the Cook
    who held her
Until any creature but Cat would have miscarried incontinent,
Was whiz'd through three circles of hell, through Stratford Broadway,
Through the Region Elenore via Steeple Bumsted to Stickey End,
And deposited with a Thump on a Kitchen Table;
While the Demon Cook, muttering dark venoms, rusht for the
    Primus,
Because that is the quickest Thing in the World to boil a Kettle,
Except bone-dry dead Twiggs, which she did not know about,
And if she had known would have condemn'd with Revilings
Since the whole Pride of the Craft revolts against pitiful Doings,
And aught uncostly, not bought or sold, they condemn as pitiful.

Releast at last, after the Tea and Gossip
Of town-Cook and Mrs. Clayfoot had flow'd to Insipidity;
Releast, but trembling, outraged, disorientated,
Musa on feverish Pads streakt for the Boothole,
Where seated in Darkness, composing Lamentations,
She fain would have deplor'd her Fate: to her Emanation
Would have accus'd the Race of Man, and against his Harlotry
Prepar'd deep Spells, and hatcht abominable Vengeance;
But that the Clayfoot, enwrapt in her Female Prudence,
(And having the Scrubbing to do) snatcht her up in a Jiffy,
And popt her out, not unkindly, at the Back, on the Drying-Green.
Trembling she croucht; but her electric Whiskers
Knew on the instant the touch of endearing Substance.
Her Eyes narrow'd; her Nostril snuft a verdurous Aroma;
She turn'd her Jowl sideways, and with her smooth cheek caress'd it,
Coarse, cutting Coxfoot-grass, the Panacea,
The Salad which is Tonick and Emetick,
And to domesticated Felines sweet and salutary.
She with immense Labour, being without true Molars,
During an Hour's Space fretted and ravell'd it,
Until the most Part of the indurated Vegetable
Had been devour'd into her urban but competent Stomach.
The Ball of hardwrought Fibres revolving in her Inwards
Shortly produc'd an Upheaval: with mighty Labour
(But not forgetting to shunt in reverse to escape the Pollution)
She return'd it to Light, and with it slough'd her Sorrows,
Voided her Venom, her Hatred of man's Harlotry,
And sate for a Space compos'd, and washing her Whiskers.

Musa then lifted her Eyes. The Time was Evening.
A Blackbird was setting his Rage at her Advent to Musick.
Small Moths swoopt by drunkenly, to be swip'd at;
In the Hedgerow the Shrew bustled by unsuspecting.
Behind her, in the bright Kitchen, she heard a Frying,
And after a Moment's Reflexion, decided 'twas Haddock.
The Young in her Womb seem'd to lie easier.
Let her but get her Bellyful of Victuals,
And a small Sup of Cow's Milk for her innoxious Night-Draught,
Let her but chuse whose bed must carry double,

All would be well; she did not dread the Morning:
She dream'd of prowling through the rustling Coppice,
Of slinking between the Hedgerow and the Stubble
In dry, large-moon'd Octobers; of May-mornings
When the lush mowing-Grass should skreen her Hunting
And with soft Dew drench her white-velvet Bosom;
Of fishing-Expeditions in the Summer
And cozy Firesides and good Beds in Winter.
Her children should be hunters of the Mole, the stack-Rat
And of all Vermin; her Apotheosis
Was come upon her; she had been translated.

THREE CHEERS FOR THE BLACK,
WHITE AND BLUE

Johnny is a long-haired Blue,
Looks a gentleman to you.
But his Ma was black and white,
Loved a dustbin, loved a fight;
And her little orphan boy,
Dressed up à la Fauntleroy,
Brushed and combed to look the part,
Has a wicked alley heart;
Swipes a titbit, smites a foe
With a fierce and expert blow;
Hands a deadly sock to those
Who interfere with his repose;
Circles round, intent to slog,
Any inoffensive dog;
Is profuse in phrases terse
And turns a ready, witty curse.
Yet he's a taking little brute,
The Bruiser in his ritzy suit.

If kindly owners can't be found,
Unwanted Kits are often drowned;
But some will send them to a Home,
Where those in want of them may come.
But these (though well-meant) Homes are such
That Kits do not enjoy them much.
A Mother-Cat is still not through
When Kits are weaned – there's more to do;
House-manners, hunting, washing, she
Will teach the youngsters thoroughly.
If taken away at six weeks old,
Or less, the kittens feel the cold;
Their tums upset, their lessons gone,
Quite suddenly left all alone,
Unwashed, untaught, unplayed-with, they
Get sick and stupid in a day.
Even if you live in a small flat,
O leave the kits with mother-cat
Three months or more; and you shall learn
According as you can discern.

From a Cats' Home we one day got
A long-haired Kit with many a spot;
A good one too; but O what fleas,
And how his snuffling snoot did wheeze,
And O how long we had to toil
With brush and comb and castor-oil,
And capsules for the hated worm,
To get the blighter into form!
And O how long his manners took,
So that he must be brought to book
With slaps and scolding twice a day
Before he'd tread the narrow way!
You see, the thing could hardly lap;
He missed his mother, poor old chap.
But he was strong, he found his feet,
Began to think his food a treat;

And (how it happened no one knew)
He simply grew and grew and grew.
Perhaps it was the ample food;
We like to think 'twas gratitude.

At three months, big as full-grown cat,
Which all the neighbours wondered at;
At six months, fourteen pounds he weighed,
Which all the other cats dismayed;
Yet undiscouraged he went on
Till pounds he numbered twenty-one
At three years old: in two years more
He made his top score, twenty-four.

It's nice to have a cat that's fat.
At least, a cat as fat as that.
He had such spreading, fubsy feet;
He had a bottom you could beat;
He loved a rough-house, and would spring
And rush about like anything.
You see, he need not be afraid,
Like small cats delicately made.
And when downstairs he'd run and jump
His feet like football-boots would thump.
We used to carry him about,
Draped round our necks, and take him out,
And those beholding him said "Cor!"
As though expecting him to roar.

He died before the beastly Blitz,
Which would have scared him into fits,
And (bar the start) his life was passed
In Fun and Games from first to last.

THE KITTEN'S ECLOGUE

Auctor

Tell now, good Kit, of three months' age, or less,
Whence dost thou bring thy perfect blessedness?
Beast which must perish, and all black to view,
What makes the happiness of such as you?

Bogey Baby

My sable hue, like Ethiopian queen,
My raven tincture and my jetty dye,
Nor as defect or blemish can be seen
By anybody who hath half an eye.
What sight more welcome than the night above?
What hue more honoured in the courts of love?

Unseen at night I ramble, being black,
And against black you will not hear me rail.
They kept the sooty whelp for fortune's sake
When all my stripy brethren plumbed the pail.
Their mice I kill, I stuff me with their tuck,
And no man kicks me lest he spoil his luck.

That sex, which some a sorry burthen deem,
I glory in, and mightily rejoice;
Though but a babe, before the fire I dream
Already that I hear my lover's voice;
What music shall I have – what dying wails –
The seldom female in a world of males!

And when love's star above the chimneys shines,
And in my heart I feel the sacred fire,
Upon the ridge-tile will I hymn these lines,
With which great Venus doth my soul inspire;
Then see the Toms, in gallant cavalcade,
Come flying to the lovesick fair one's aid!

What mortal dame, what merely human she,
What strong enchantress could thus honoured sit;
What maid could draw her suitors on like me,
Sing such a tune, and get away with it?
What charmer could men's souls so nearly touch?
What nymph, I ask, could do one half as much?

Hold me not foul for that I wanton be;
These amorous frolics are but innocence;
I court no tickle immortality,
And fear no judgment when I go from hence;
No hope, no dread my little grave contains,
Nor anything beside my scant remains!

Bogey Baby's Emblem: O felis semper felix!

Everybody Else's Emblem: Mud.

THE MATRON-CAT'S SONG

So once again the trouble's o'er,
    And here I sit and sing;
Forgetful of my paramour
    And the pickle I was in:
Lord, lord, it is a trying time
    We bear when we're expecting,
When folk reproach us for the crime
    And frown with glance correcting.
So purra wurra, purra wurra, pronkum pronkum;
    Purra wurra, pronkum, pronkum purr.

How much I feared my kits would be
    Slain in the hour of birth!
And so I sought a sanctuary
    Which causes me some mirth;

The surly cook, who hates all cats,
    Hath here a little closet,
And here we nest among her hats –
    Lord save me when she knows it!

Four kits have I of aspect fair,
    Though usually but three;
Two female tabs, a charming pair,
    Who much resemble me;
Lord, lord, to think upon the sport
    Which doth await the hussies;
They'll be no better than they ought,
    Nor worse than other pussies.

Yet as becomes a mother fond
    I dote upon my boys,
And think they will excel beyond
    All other toms in noise;
How harsh their manly pelts will be,
    How stern and fixed each feature –
If they escape that cruelty
    Which man doth work on nature!

Those eyes which now are sealèd fast
    Nine days against the light
Shall ere few months are overpast
    Like stars illume the night;
Those voices that with feeble squall,
    Demand my whole attention,
Shall earn with rousing caterwaul
    Dishonourable mention.

But then, alas, I shall not care
    How flighty they may be,
For ere they're grown I'll have to bear
    Another four, or three;
And after all, they are the best
    While the whole crew reposes

With fast-shut eyes, weak limbs at rest,
  And little wrinkled noses.
So purra wurra, purra wurra, pronkum pronkum:
  Purra wurra pronkum, pronkum ryestraw:
Pronkum ryestraw, pronkum ryestraw,
  Pur-ra – wur-ra – pron-kum
Pronk . . . Foof.
                    (She sleeps.)

              . . . and with this humble image of
                  fulfilment and repose,
                  reader, we come to

                  THE END

THE ERMINE

I know this Ermine. He is small,
Keen-biting, very quick withal.

He dies of soil. He is the snow.
I marvel anyone can know

This Ermine: he is delicate.
Yet, maculate immaculate,

He is well seen and known by me,
Rough-handed homespun though I be.

I muse on him. His little eye
Reflects no beam I do not spy.

I through his snowy silence hear
Beyond the labyrinthine ear.

Royal he is. What makes him so?
Why, that too is a thing I know:

It is his blame, his black, his blot;
The badge of kings, the sable spot.

O subtle, royal Ermine, tell
Me how to wear my black as well.

THE NEOPHYTE

Something I see and feel,
But I must not speak.
It lives, O it is real,
But cold and weak
As a far light in a cave,
As the faint glow
That the green glow-worms have,
As stars of snow;
As tenuous jellies small,
Knotted, turned in,
That you may see on a wall
Where the tide has been;
Whence the great swinging deep,
With its bell-mouthed roar,
Has gone, and left them asleep,
Flowers no more;
Has gone, falling away
Far to the main:
But with the day, with the new day,
Shall come again.

THE TREE AT DAWN

How lonely is the birth of day –
    The day that shall be full
Of men and beasts, of work and play; .
    How silent and how cool
The rising of the tyrant sun,
    When steeped in vapour dim,
The moths of night drift grey and dun,
    Not yet in awe of him.

In the cold grey, and all alone,
    I left my useless bed:
I fetched the hook, I fetched the stone,
    From the dark, littered shed;
And while the dew would serve my turn
    I cut the nettles strong,
The mowing-grass and parsley-fern
    The garden hedge along.

How lonely seem the creatures then;
    How lonely, even trees;
But the conceiving minds of men
    Are lonelier than these;
The throstle-cock but half awake,
    The moss-rose in a mood
Millions of summers old, can make
    No claim to solitude:

They do not know themselves alone,
    And knowing would not care;
But holiness invests each one
    In the grey morning air;
Their being wraps them all around,
    Their love is plain to see,
When there is not a single sound,
    And not a soul but me.

When there is not a single sound –
    For by the dewy hedge
I let the stone fall to the ground,
    I cease my sacrilege;
Still as a plant I stand, and look,
    And now no longer break
The breathing silence with my hook,
    But watch the colours wake.

The great bole of the ancient tree
    Is glittering green ore,
And dark green as the deepest sea
    His boughs secrete and store
The spirit of the dreadful night,
    While glowing as the gleed
The lingering fruits burn in the light
    Of their last dawn, and bleed.

But innocent; for all the pain
    Is in me who behold,
And mine, not his, the crimson stain,
    And mine the goblin gold
That glances where the lichens grow,
    And mine the fruits that bless,
And mine, where fallen brown they sow
    New trees, or rottenness.

But his that life mysterious,
    And sacred, as I well see,
And well companioned; glorious
    Beyond the great old tree
The pale-blue velvet cabbages
    Stand lovely as a dream,
And violet and pink sweet-peas
    Clearer begin to gleam,

With white that glimmered long ago,
        When from my bed I came.
But look, the clouds begin to glow,
        The east begins to flame;
The god leaps up, the day is here,
        The heat pours from the sky:
The tree is commonplace and dear,
        And I am only I.

REFLECTION AFTER VICTORY

Whom shall we envy, of all who live in the ruins?

Burdened, I envy the man who sets down his burden,
Compendious kitbag of troubles,
On the worn floor of the cheap cottage, his haven,
His last harbour but one. He is old;
Glad to be old, for the struggle is over;
Poor, and glad to be poor, for that is simple:
Need meditate no journeys, for he can afford none,
And the one that remains will be taken care of by others.
He is solitary, his friends are dead or departed;
That is melancholy, but no worse; they were not his treasure;
That was always beyond. Will he find it here?

He is tired. The place is deserted, and rain is falling.
The bit of cold food, set out by some village woman,
Is there, and the flimsy kettle boils on the old grate.
He eats and drinks absently, soothed by the rainy twilight,
Goes and lies down on the bed in the little dim room,
Covers himself with a blanket. The water drips
From the pipe to the barrel, drowsy and musical;
The wood-dove croons in the wet. He is sleeping,
Lulled at last from the pain of life, and the weary
Search for the lost supreme, the crown and the rainbow.

Visit him there, O cruel elusive;
Peace be on him, whether of hopeless grave
Or of light at the last; which shall bless him, the rose,
Young moss-rose that smiles in the sun, or this, the gipsy
Nightshade, dull flower and fruit of blackness?

THE GREAT WINTER,
1946-1947

The leaves die, fall and go.
They lie all under the snow.
In the great snow the grass dies;
Still the deep clouds fill the skies.
Summer wept, and now the east
Roaring falls on man and beast.

And man and beast die, fall and go,
Under the sky's pall, rain or snow;
Neither hut nor palace stays
The sure ending of their days;
Age and sickness and the wars
Stretch them stiff beneath the stars.

And the stars die, fall and go.
Eye by eye, they cease to glow;
Orb by orb, the storm of suns
To its end in glory runs;
The great wheels, the galaxies,
Shall turn no more about the skies.

Since all must die, fall and go,
Why do we mourn that it is so?
All mourn, lament and weep
That creation falls asleep?
This was given us to make
Our spirits homeless for His sake.

THE STOLEN BABE

There's trouble in the sky; hear the trees groaning!
I don't know these parts, maybe I've lost my way.
I never saw that house before – smile, my pretty!
And I don't like the look of it – let's be getting on.
The great dark trees look to me like trouble,
Clouds are the wrong shape, and the rocks are too old.
O deary me, if I only had a cottage,
Perhaps I could do right and bring ye up lovely.
But I keep on walking into bad unlucky places,
Through the cold wind that the flowers are a-dying of,
Into bombed-out places and places full of soldiers,
Bad places full of people, bad places where there ain't any.

Why did they leave ye alone in that garden?
Ah, that was a lovely place, though it was lonely.
Lovely foreign flowers, better than roses,
And you, my lily, the whitest in the world!
And I that have gone all my life dark and lonely
Felt the dark in my blood and the lonely nights and days,
And I took ye for a charm-like against the darkness,
To keep me safe in the bad unlucky places,
Where there's things that ain't right, and them sad voices.

For you stretched out your little arms to me, my lovey,
And you smiled in my face as though you were my own.
I think now and then of them that's lost ye,
But what do I care for all their trouble?
I know ye've no mother, I see it in your face.
When ye don't smile, it looks right mournful.
Smile at me now, my sweet white lily!

Ah, I know she's ailing, that's what kills me.
She's not like us, and I don't know what to do.
I'd take her to a hospital, but I don't trust 'em.
Besides, she's so white, they'd know I'd stole her.
Ah sleep, my lovey! sleep, my lily!

Tired to death she is, but she ain't crying;
She's one of them that's too proud to complain.

Let's sit down, here in the churchyard.
See the green grass and the flowers on the graves!
There's a baby's head on that old stone there –
Smiling, smiling, between the little wings,
Smiling in the darkness under the yew.
There's a pretty bee, she's going home now,
Home to her little burrow under the stone.
Ah, she's the lucky one, she's got a deep shelter,
Out of the cold wind, out of the rain,
Out of the bad luck under the ground:
A good safe place, baby, under the ground.

THE OTHER

Like a bird in the rainy cover
      When song is fallen still,
It dwells apart, and over
      Blue hill upon blue hill.

As a bird in the green places
      When summer days are long,
Falls weary, and embraces
      Silence instead of song,

Far and apart it muses
      In the obscure and dim,
Forgetting the sweet uses
      Of voice and feather and limb.

Small, small and slender,
      Crowned with its faint gold crown,
It dwells where the light is tender,
      Like fair hair falling down.

215

Swiftness and song were moulded
   Into that wing, that breast;
But now the wing is folded,
   The throbbing throat at rest.

When from that bosom narrow
   The fiery singing flew,
Like a sharp secret arrow
   It pierced my armour through.

But its great silence haunts me
   In the solemn summer gloom;
The voiceless thing enchants me
   As with a sense of doom.

A monument, a token
   Of all we have betrayed,
Of all that we have broken –
   It makes my soul afraid.

Far from the tumult fleeing,
   The shrines that we destroy,
Is it my own grieved being
   Mourning its unborn joy,

Or some indignant spirit
   Whose power can afford
To give us what we merit –
   A silence like a sword?

HERDING LAMBS

To O.

In the spring, in the morning,
We heard the high bleat,
And the low voice of the ewes, and the rainlike
Rustle of feet.

In the daffodil day
My sister called to me,
And out to the garden gate
We went to see.

No dogs, no sticks,
No shouting, no noise,
Only the rustle, the bleating,
The chirping boys.

Slowly they moved along,
Herded by three
Old grey men, and five children,
To the fresh lea.

And when a silly lamb
Turned back in fright
A withered or an infant hand
Guided him right.

The early mist muffled their sound,
Muted that double chime
Trembling along the grassy ground
From the morning of time.

THE CAPTIVE BIRD OF PARADISE

Give me the bird of Paradise, though dying,
Exiled and doomed, ravished from the Elysian
Forest where I shall never see it flying,
Where Cœlogyne flowers like a vision:
Never shall hear the love-tormented crying.

For there abides the torrent of golden wire,
The silver silk, the cactus-anther river,
The rose-death purple mantled on with fire,
The dying-dolphin green where lightnings quiver.
The trembling arches of the silent lyre.

Though I shall never see the sudden turning
Into a sphery monstrance, globe of splendour,
The ecstasy that is beyond our learning,
The action and the attitude that render
Love back to whence it came, the phoenix burning:

Though I shall never hear, rending asunder
The bonds that trammel love, that cry of passion,
The voice that is more terrible than thunder:
Though at its death my life be desolation,
Give me the bird of paradise, the wonder.

THE WORLD IS HOLLOW

Father, they told me that the world is hollow,
      A thing no child believes,
While the young fruit swells, and the swallow
      Goes hawking round the eaves;
For though, since it is human, the child grieves,
      Hope is its kingdom, and the mortal future
      Holds love, the captain-jewel of the creature.

218

And it is well that no child should despair;
      For if that visage rose
Before him, lighted by the desert glare
      From the heart's sleeping snows;
If that intolerable vision froze
      His spirit, he must be the snow-queen's prize,
      Trying to spell *eternity* in ice.

But man's despair is like the Arabian sun,
      When the last morning cloud
Melts in the fire; then the lost wretch alone,
      Whom nothing bends to shroud,
Falls in the sand, and cries his need aloud,
      Full-grown at last to love, when he can find
      No cloud, no rock, no shelter in the mind.

Hollow the world, and never to be filled
      Save by the One supreme.
Despair, that burning angel, by the child
      Unperceived even in dream,
Stands sentinel by Eden, and the beam
      Unmitigated, doom pronounced by light,
      Glares from his arms, and blinds the earthly sight.

THE CEDAR

Look from the high window with the eye of wonder
When the sun soars over and the moon dips under.

Look when the sun is coming and the moon is going
On the aspiring creature, on the cedar growing.

Plant or world? are those lights and shadows
Branches, or great air-suspended meadows?

Boles and branches, haunted by the flitting linnet,
Or great hillsides rolling up to cliffs of granite?

Those domed shapes, thick-clustered on the ledges,
Upright fruit, or dwellings thatched with sedges?

Fair through the eye of innocence returning,
This is a country hanging in the morning;

Scented alps, where nothing but the daylight changes,
Climbing to black walls of mountain ranges;

And under the black walls, under the sky-banners,
The dwellings of the blessed in the green savannahs.

HILL AND VALLEY

To D.C.

High on dry hills, I think I hear the mow
Falling with whispers where the land is low,
Down in lush aits and meadows where the willows grow,
Down by deep drinking-places where the cattle go.

I watch in silence, while the lark is shrill,
Drifting grape-coloured shadows on the hill,
Drifting stone-coloured sheep cropping and roving,
The long-abiding and the ever-moving.

I think I could mind the sheep on the hill for ever,
And then again it seems
As though I were made to live by a great river,
Watching the cattle drinking in dimpled gleams,
Winding the wands of willow that spring by the streams.

THE FATHER QUESTIONED

My mind alights like a bird in the dark tree.
Now in this rain the old cones will be falling,
But I will think of them new in their spring silver,
Silver under the waxen green netted with rose,
Like rare pale luminous shells adorning
The solemn deep-sea levels of heavy boughs.
Dead father, your bones lie under the cedar.

O tell me what was meant by the sun's affliction.
The raw new sorrowful houses, the unmade road
Saddened the sun. O but my heart was heavy!
How could such sadness be? for love had fled them
Even from the foundation; they blasphemed
The deep deep Law; they cried abomination.

Sad in the sun, the road drooped down to the sea.
The hot salt slipway glaring in desolation
Remembered the woe of the sea. The screaming bird
Swooped on its offal, my soul. The unreturning
Haunted the quays. What was that place, dead father,
And did you too mourn by that shore of sorrow?

The spectral gaslight of the wet street in winter
Was the pale squalid banner of man's affliction.
O father, who was the noseless man, and the child
With angel eyes and face all covered with sores?
What was the woman screaming? why did they take her
Away, and where? had someone hurt her, father?

The unemployed are marching, singing of hunger.
Why are they hungry? the shops are full of food;
Why can't they have it? Now they've turned into soldiers,
And must fight and die. Why must they die, dead father?
Who says they cannot have food, and then says 'Die'?

But as for the hyacinth, crocus, daphne,
They speak so plainly, do not ask an answer.
The sweet smell, gentle form, and gallant shining
Are what we seek: why is the rest not so?
Swift to the heart comes the poor plant's kind legend,
Like a strong word for ever lucid, faithful.
The dropping woodbine in the rainy hedgerow,
That was my love; and the young yellow sallow,
And the gold-spangled birch-tree's scarlet mushroom.
But you spoke on of the world's ills, dead father.

Father, there is something I cannot tell you.
There are no words. It lives behind the sky.
It is there in the tree, and in some people's faces,
Like music, like the lily of the valley,
Like a green grave and like a happy morning:
O, even in the grass, even in dew.
Did you too seek it, did you try to find it?
Perhaps have found it, for I feel the answer
Steal through the blood and bone of your begetting.
Speak to me through the blood, my living father.

Child, that is love that lives behind the sky,
Yourself sought weeping, orphaned, sore lamenting,
The music and the lily of the valley
Are the vile houses and the desolate harbour,
The sad, the hungry men, the howling charging
Infantry, and the general despair.
The noseless man, the mad-drunk woman screaming,
Are the clean crocus and voluptuous daphne,
And the sore child the delicate woodbine springing.
It is you who make them one. That is your treasure.
Can you seize earth and heaven by the two horns
And bend and string them? Can you be that Eros?

The child must understand the sun's affliction;
Green grave, and weeping night, and happy morning.

PENITENCE

To G.H.

Like rain in the young corn,
Bridal and blessed rain,
So late, so timely born
Out of long lack and pain,
Out of the heavy sky
Smitten by fire,
Fathered by lightning, by
The bolt of heaven's desire:

Called down by bitter need,
Sent down by divine law
To save the blade and the seed:
Love leaps to send and draw
Sweet water got by fire
Out of a cloudy grief;
Sweet dew of strong desire
To save the flower and the leaf.

DEW

Secret and still, as the light goes,
Soundless the dew falls, not like rain:
Freshness of violet, richness of rose,
Bloom on the blade of the green grain,
Misty and waxen veil of the beautiful heath,
Incense-tear from the cedar, weeping its balm,
Pearl on the cheek of the peach, film of the breath
Of the cold night coming with gradual calm;
Dew with the stillness, dew with the chill of death,
Falling in failing light, as the voices cease;
Dew, the water of life, the pardon, the peace.

223

A WORN THEME

Fairest is soonest gone –
But O gone where?
When we are left alone,
When rainbows faint in air,

When that light on the sea
Dies in a leaden shade,
And after the one bee
The bells of azure fade,

Where has the spirit fled,
Whence did it come?
Ah, when a beauty is dead
Its soul goes home.

Then let us go there too;
Dearly I long to be
Where lives the vanished blue,
The moment's light at sea,

The smiles and the tender graces,
All gone by,
The flowers and the faces
That were born but to die.

Let us go, let us go
To their immortal day,
For all we have to do
Is to be fair as they,
And die, and flee away.

NARROW BUT DEEP

Poor man I used to meet sometimes
On Sunday 'buses in the war,
Who missed the sound of the church chimes,
Heard faintly in the field afar
Or roaring where the sallies swung;
Quiet man, wherever now you are,
With such calm speech and simple tongue:

With widowed, unrebellious mind,
With an old, childlike, steadfast face,
So free from passion, yet so kind,
Unlearned, but without a trace
Of ignorance, enemy to grace:
As the long bombers' night loomed down,
And the crammed, stinking 'bus would race
Back to the cowering, helpless town:

You lit the chapel of your life,
With its scrubbed floor and rough white wall;
You closed me in from bitter strife,
You raised the light perpetual
Above your little altar; all
Your long obedience shone on me:
Darkling beneath the double pall
Of night and sorrow, I could see.

Hemmed in by a strait holiness,
Much deeper ran my shallow tide;
Those walls, as saving arms may press
A child from harm on either side,
Shut out my pain, shut out my pride;
And now and then a look would come –
So clear, I thought that I descried
The mother and the cottage home.

OLD CLOCKWORK TIME

Old clockwork Time beats in his tower,
I hear his wintry, wheezing breath;
His faded face looks down; a flower
Answers *Eternity* beneath.

The seconds creak, the quarters chime,
The light dust falls, the heavy doom;
Dead dust and brazen bells of time
Are younger than those bells of bloom.

He beats his anvil, and his blood
Moves to its measured pulses still:
That humble angel carved in wood
Looks up to its immortal hill.

With moveless, dedicated eyes
It gazes on, while all the waste
Seconds and minutes, hours and days
Plunge to that echoing gulf, the past.

Held, like a perfume held in air,
Or smiling from a nameless mound,
What does each Adoration care
For sorrow measured off by sound?

THE LAMMASTIDE FLOWER

Now that the man is in his grave,
Now that the child is dead and gone,
Now that the summer wanes, and all
Is housed or rotting, there again
I see the yellow toadflax wave
And wiry harebell over stone;
While like a weary prodigal
Man counts the harvest of his pain.

You yellow spires of Lammastide
That look not at me but beyond;
You silent bells that mirror sky
Yet hang so meekly to the ground;
What, either far or deep descried,
Holds you so rapt, in such a bond,
One looking low, one looking high:
What is that silence you have found?

The yellow toadflax said, "Be still.
I see the Powers, they see me,
I see those Two, and both are gold:
Two golds in one, and both are true.
I gaze, but cannot gaze my fill.
I can but look, I can but be,
I can but speak it as of old."
The vaulted harebell, "In the blue".
"Two golds", they said, and "In the blue".

THE TUFT OF VIOLETS

Our solitary larch
Spread her green silk against the south,
When late-relenting March
Ended the sowing-time of welcome drouth;
And from the bank beneath
Sheltered by budding hedge and bowing tree,
A moist delicious breath
Of rainy violets came out to me.

There was the healthy mass
Of dark delightful leaves, with their own breath
Of silvan moss and grass;
But all among and over them there went

The sweetness lovers know,
And age will pause upon, while time returns,
And earlier violets grow
In a lost kingdom where no creature mourns.

From high above my head
The mated missel-thrush was singing proudly,
And through that dusky bed
The light-reflecting bee rejoicing loudly,
Kissing each modest face,
Sang to them well how beautiful they were,
Who in that slight embrace
Let fall upon the green a little tear.

Time ceased, as if the spring
Had been eternity; I had no age;
The purple and the wing
That visited and hymned it, were a page
Royally dyed, written in gold;
Royal with truth, for ever springing;
For ever, as of old,
The sunlight and the darkness and the singing.

AGED MAN TO YOUNG MOTHER

Now he is here, he needs a friend.
Cover him from the dreadful light.
Weak from the nightmare journey,
Cast out of his heaven,
Thrown naked on a bitter shore,
Hide his eyes awhile from space,
Break the news gently about time,
Help him to forget:
To forget exile and death,
Crass defeat and the repulse
From joys he thought his own for ever,

In the place of dreaming, beautiful island,
Where the dream and the life are one.
Ah, can you know, you so young,
Even you, his island home,
You that bore him in the night,
The bitterness of birth and death?

Did you learn, did you listen,
So that you keep in mind for ever
Hope and anguish both together?
We need a friend. Whisper to us
Close in the ear, about God's mercy;
Whisper, "I love you. Love is here."
Hold hard the lonely, bending hand,
The hook that seeks a mooring,
The roseleaf hand or parchment claw;
And put your hand
Under the skull, comfort the neck;
Poor neck; it aches more than it knows
With traffic to and from the brain.

Dark journeys, all alone,
Coming or going, and hard
Throes for all to endure, mother;
We all need pity. O give us
Pity from prescient hands and eyes,
Pity for all from the sacred breast,
From the low voice in the dark
When morning is far, and fear
Bellows in the cold caves
Deep under the mind of man.

Come to meet us. Think of our need.
Plan out the rescue. That stringent pain
Gave you a glimpse of the iron passes,
The basalt walls they forget. O mother,
Light us, coming or going,
Bring us the Mercy.
So when the night is over,

So when day is no more,
We shall forget, and be merry,
Dancing and singing in tune and time,
In time, and beyond time;
And you – you shall smile at our dancing and singing.
You did not fail us. We are your own.

TRUE ISRAEL

On his deathbed as he lies,
David in his cradle dies,
For he was too poor to go
About this huge distracting show
To see the jubilee and woe:
And his learning was not such
As to bring him very much
Where the sophistries are made
And the early colours fade.
Aged, he is going hence
In his pristine innocence:
If you would describe his lot
You must tell what he had not.
Planted in an alien place,
Parted from the timeless grace
That like attar long-abiding
Haunts and hovers, lies in hiding
In its ancient cradle still,
In the city on the hill;
Orphaned, disinherited,
Free, but free among the dead.
Yet you must rehearse as well
That he was true Israel;
Though his body could not thrive,
Yet he saved his soul alive.
Sumptuously he would rejoice
In splendour, being poor by choice:

Humble, he could be intent
On the real Magnificent:
His charity was like the air,
Unwounded round him everywhere.
So there is no need to pity
His poor bones in this dire city,
For his loves shall come like bees,
And wrap his relics as they please;
Cere him sweet on busy wings,
And bury David with the kings.

HEN UNDER BAY-TREE

A squalid, empty-headed Hen,
Resolved to rear a private brood,
Has stolen from the social pen
To this, the noblest solitude.

She feels this tree is magical.
She knows that spice, beneath her breast
That sweet dry death; for after all
Her cradle was the holy East.

Alert she sits, and all alone;
She breathes a time-defying air:
Above her, songbirds many a one
Shake the dark spire, and carol there.

Unworthy and unwitting, yet
She keeps love's vigil glorious;
Immovably her faith is set,
The plant of honour is her house.

SIX DREAMS AND A VISION

All life is strange:
Waking no less than sleeping; all
Mantled in mystery of perpetual change,
Like the ephemeral
Blushings and whitenings of a wasting fire.
But the white fear, the blushes of desire,
The ashes and the embers and the air,
Black coal, blue boding flame,
They build us palaces without a name,
We write our timeless, spaceless histories there,
And read ourselves, before we are quite spent,
In that more swiftly wasting element.

But there's the story of the Salamander,
And the man who looked at the sky,
And shifting sands and brooks that wander
And the way twigs lie;
They may say things silently:
And the toothless babe may speak
To resolve the mother's doubt;
The cat and dog and ass call out,
The strong be guided by the weak;
The powers can use a little leaf
As a simple to heal grief;
Simple or symbol; and a dream
Be more than what such things may seem.

A Stranger and a Sojourner

Always the unknown place,
The place where I have not been.
Always an unknown face
In a strange scene;
Always the people whom I do not know,
In a mysterious land.
Sometimes tall houses over the treacherous flow

Of streams that scoop the sand
And hollow out the solid-seeming stone,
Till beautiful abodes
Totter above foundations nearly gone,
And ruined roads
Crumble and fall: and I am not afraid,
But think, in my dream,
A little sadly, as the waves invade
Dressed stone and beam,
Fall then, fine house: to the dark dust, white stone.
There is no shelter here. I will go on.

But although the houses fall
And the road fails under the feet,
Life can live outside a wall;
There is life where never yet
Air blew or water ran,
Where time is not a tragic theme,
Where the misery of man
Has not cast his bitter dream;
Where unfallen spirits rest
Like the swan upon her nest,
Moated round with innocence,
Further than the stars from hence;
Whence arrayed like her they shall
Come gliding on the clear canal,
By the lonely waterside,
Clothed in a pride that is not pride:
And suddenly in that still place
Making all sail, as if to embrace
All that creation holds of fair,
Tower to the clearer, lonelier air.

Forms with Infinite Meaning

There was a dawn
In a grey land that was not sorrowful.
Simple and cool

The low smooth hills stood decent and withdrawn;
And somewhere in the dimness there were shells.
Whether small shells, and near,
Or mighty shells reared up before the hills,
I do not know; but dear,
Dear with a worth beyond all earthly price,
And clothed upon with such significance
That their melodious stillness was a dance.
And then there came a voice,
And up the clean sky rushed a whiter sun,
And there was done
Some great solemnity, which yet was play.
In that strange dream my heart kept holiday;
Forms more than forms are shadowed in my mind,
My loves for ever, though of alien kind.

The Tree

Once in a dream I came
And stood, and into a hollow I looked down.
What were those flowers of flame,
Hanging so still, unblown,
Pendent upon a great and great-leaved tree
In the deep-shadowed glade before the door
Of the veiled cavern? Shade perpetually
Lay timeless on the unstirred forest floor;
In a strange fear
And trembling in the silence, I drew near.

Vast was that tree,
And its leaves huge, and its whole aspect still.
O still as sleep, and sleep itself to me
It seemed beside that hollow in the hill:
And I stole on, and saw,
Pendent from stalks, those flowers that were men,
Asleep, and beautiful; beheld them draw
Their light, tranced breath – I wept with gladness then,
For I had feared to find that they were dead.

And their fantastic garments were of red,
Blue, green, and cloth of metal: ivory
Their sleeping faces in the shadowy tree.
This was a blessed people not yet come to be.

A Vision of Extreme Delight

Another people dwelt under a sky
Dark as our midnight but intensely blue;
Against it luminously
Waved palmlike forests of the very hue
That shines unearthly in our glaciers
(To us so mineral and miser-cold),
Melting into the green the glow-worm bears;
But pulsing with a life untold,
Waving with rapture in dark windless air,
Growing and sinking even as I gazed.
Creatures were moving there,
So blessed, I forgot to be amazed.
I saw no limbs or features. In the night
They showed like monoliths of living ice,
Streaming with rays of visible delight.
O there is no device
Of language for them; but if I were blind
I should still see palms waving without wind,
And living jewels, cataracts of bliss,
Against the dark of other skies than this.

The Transparent Earth

Earth is bowed with a weight
Hard and heavy to bear;
Bowed and curved round the great
Core of despair.
Go into a deep cave,
Where the stone groans in the dark
Like a voice in the grave;

235

Lift up the light, and mark
The heavy sag of the stone,
Bearing its load of woe
Till time shall be undone
And the aching form can go.
Earth is weary and old,
So men have always said;
Earth is heavy and cold,
On the cold breasts of the dead.

But in sleep I saw her, clear
As a drop of dew:
Like a crystal was her sphere,
And the sun shone through:
Standing at midnight in the street
I saw the sun between my feet,
Shining up into my face
Through earth colourless as space;
Through an earth as clear as wine,
Colourless and crystalline.

But My Neighbour is My Treasure

Solemn and lovely visions and holy dreams,
Mysterious portents, wanderers who range
Among unearthly themes,
Strong catalysts that change
The colours and the contours of the mind;
Be silent in your valleys in the moon,
Fade to the country that we never find:
For I am listening for that mortal tune,
The broken anthem of my fallen kind,
And seeking for the vision of those I see
Daily and here, in this poor house with me.

Their name is Wonderful, a holy name;
These in the light of heaven I shall behold,
If I can come there, standing in the flame

Of glory, with the blessed in their gold.
There is no dream more wonderful, for they
Are worth the whole creation, each alone.
Grant me to see their beauty on that Day!
There is no vision to prefer, but One.

The Great and Terrible Dream

Dark valley, or dark street: arches or trees
Or rocks? Shadow of evening, or of cloud?
Fear in the air, and a profound unease;
Then panic-driven feet, and from a shroud
Of dust or darkness, ravings as of men
Running in horror from some sight so dire
That the flesh cannot stay, or turn again,
But mindless flees, as hand is snatched from fire.
Fixed in pure terror, horribly afraid,
I listened to that frenzied multitude;
And a calm solemn voice behind me said,
In answer to my thought, *They fear the blood.*
Then in the dream my heart within my breast
Struck hugely stroke on stroke, driving me on
As a ship's engine drives her to the east
Against the eastern gale: Love was alone
And in extremity! Into the crowd
I hurled myself, and fought against the stream
As frantic mothers fight, who hear a loud
Scream from a burning house, an infant's scream.
Men plunged and hurtled by me, without mind,
Ants from a broken anthill, all infused
With one atrocious instinct, fierce and blind.
And wounded, naked, trampled, torn and bruised
I fought against them for a weary time,
Willing to die before my heart should break;
I thought them murderers fleeing from their crime,
And what they feared so madly, I must seek.

Then it was over: then there were no more
Opposing, then the tumult of those men
Ceased, as when sound is cut off by a door
Closing; and all but darkness filled the glen,
Or street, or vaulted place; so silence fell.
And the voice spoke again as solemnly
Behind me; calmly the invisible
Said, *He is there. Look on Him. That is He.*

The fear of death came on me. (Long ago
I saw men carrying a coffin by;
They stumbled, the lid moved; and horror so
Wrung me, that I fell without a cry,
And blackness roared upon me; but in vain,
The shell was empty.) Torn with love and awe,
I saw the Face, the plaited thorns, the stain
Of blood descending to the beard I saw;
And felt the power of life conquering death,
More dread than death, for death is vincible.
It struck me down. It stopped the very breath
Itself had given. But the dream was well:

O well is me, and happy shall I be!
Look! He is there. Look on Him. That is He.

THE NEW HOUSE

Older than the house, the south-west wails;
And the strong new house, like a house in the old tales,
Is nothing but desire and fear forming and dissolving,
With the wind streaming, with the world revolving.

As in the old tales strong houses vanish
When broken promises and murder banish
Bright walls to limbo, and leave but the bare heather,
So we and the house are vanishing altogether:

238

Save for the love that life always remembers,
Telling the tale over the winter embers;
Save for the love moving this hand over the paper,
Hand that must soon vanish to earth and vapour.

IN THE OPEN

Move into the clear.
Keep still, take your stand
Out in the place of fear
On the bare sand;

Where you have never been,
Where the small heart is chilled;
Where a small thing is seen,
And can be killed.

Under the open day,
So weak and so appalled,
Look up and try to say,
Here I am, for you called.

You must haunt the thin cover
By that awful place,
Till you can get it over
And look up into that face.

THE IRISH PATRIARCH

He bathes his soul in women's wrath;
His whiskers twinkle, and it seems
As if he trod some airy path
In that young land of warriors' dreams;
As if he took a needle-bath
In mountain falls, in tingling streams.

The man whom nagging drives to drink
Should learn from him, whom female rage
Seems but to make a precious link
With some sweet ancient heritage,
With women saying – huh! – what they think!
To the amusement of the sage.

O women, what a boon it is,
With workday worries at their worst,
When hordes of little miseries
Force us to speak our mind or burst,
To be Rich-angered Mistresses,
Not Shrews and Vixens, Cross and Curst!

THREE FEMININE THINGS

Female Yew-tree, shedding condensed drops of transpired water
See how my yew-tree
In utter drought and heat
Breeds kindness in blindness,
Drops dew about her feet;
How she in beauty,
She in her ancient calm,
Stands sleeping, stands weeping
Her penitential balm.

Like that poor widow
Who gave her livelihood,
Since living is giving,
She sheds her stainless blood;
From holy shadow,
Dark mourning that she wears,
Comes coolness in fulness,
Come drops as warm as tears.

Poor young woman

> Sorrow and weakness
> Lie heavy on this maid;
> Small earnings, great yearnings –
> She loves, but is afraid;
> Here she in meekness,
> She in her poor attire,
> Sits sewing, unknowing
> The end of her desire.
>
> But that poor rapture,
> Like a thin eager root,
> Could flourish, could nourish
> Some blessed leaf or shoot;
> Or tower to the capture,
> Like eagle in the air,
> And singing, come bringing
> An angel by the hair.

Evening Star

> The last vermilion
> Smoulders along the west
> Horizon, to blazon
> The dead day's arms and crest
> On that pavilion,
> Clear-hung with lucent green,
> Where growing, where glowing,
> The Planet stands, the queen.
>
> Pearl in the hollow
> Height of the sun's void throne,
> Fast sinking, but linking
> The eye to splendour gone;
> Faithfully follow,
> Bearing a blessed name;
> Still turning, still burning
> With white reflected flame.

241

CHARITY AND ITS OBJECT

Of one thing Mrs Crow was sure;
She knew for certain she was poor.
It therefore followed with perfect clarity
That she was eligible for charity.
She did not beg; she did not whine;
She only took a reasoned line;
She followed what she had been taught.
She knew that richer people ought
To help God's good deserving cases,
And so she told them to their faces.
And, merely at her mild request,
The people gave her of their best,
Glad to find one who would receive
So kindly what they had to give.
Firm in religion, there she stood,
And helped her neighbours to be good.

MOTHS AND MERCURY-VAPOUR LAMP

Some beat the glass as if in agony,
The pattern never still enough to see;
In the unearthly strong cold radiance
Eyes glitter, wings are flourished, weapons glance,
Furs, metals, dyes; duellers with flashing foils
Glitter like fire and struggle in the toils
Of potent light, as deep-sea fish are drawn
From profound dark to anguish and the dawn.

But others stand, abide the passionate sight,
All pricked and sprinkled with inhuman light,
All charactered as from sidereal
Regions, where our writ does not run at all;
And these are messengers, of whom I ask,
As I look up at moments from my task,

"What? Why? Who sends? and what is said to me
In urgent characters that I can see
And wonder at, yet never read the tongue?"
And night by night the airy envoys throng,
Solemnly habited, winged but still, and gazing
Fixedly into that furnace, that amazing
Supernal sepulchre of other light,
Born like a comet in their native night,
A final flower, a strong and deadly plant,
Forbidden by the unseen adamant.

Mysteriously attired in light and dust,
Draped in funereal splendour, like august
Mummies, authentic in a spectral grace,
Breastplate of gold, and golden mask on face,
Wing within wing, fold within fold of shroud,
Ashy and frosty cerements, and a cloud
Of the fine bloomy powder of decay,
With eyes of night or diamond turned my way,
Upright, as crucified upon the glass,
That strong invisible they cannot pass,
For ever watching at the terrible gate,
Until the writing shall be read, they wait.

CRUMBS FOR THE BIRD

Sighing we eat our doubtful bread,
Made of far-fetched and foreign grain;
Food of a kind, but somehow dead,
Being bought and sold and sold again.

But hear the painted chaffinch call;
He knows the time, and he will come;
Down from the willow-bough will fall
And gaily gather every crumb.

Then not so doubtful, not so dead,
The alien corn appears to be;
For love still sanctifies the bread
Perfection begs of poverty.

THE HEART'S DESIRE IS FULL OF SLEEP

The heart's desire is full of sleep,
For men who have their will
Have gained a good they cannot keep,
And must go down the hill

Not questioning the seas and skies,
Not questioning the years;
For life itself has closed their eyes,
And life has stopped their ears.

But some, true emperors of desire,
True heirs to all regret,
Strangers and pilgrims, still enquire
For what they never get;

For what they know is not on earth
They seek until they find;
The children hopeful in their mirth,
The old but part resigned.

And though they cannot see love's face
They tread his former track;
They know him by his empty place,
They know him by their lack.

I seek the company of such,
I wear that worn attire;
For I am one who has had much,
But not the heart's desire.

TAWNY OWL IN FIR-TREE

I hear sighing, mother Cybele;
Cave and sea voices in your cold dark tree.
Sighing and swaying voices, as the wave
Of a cold wind, like water filling a cave,
Lifts the weight of a bough as breath lifts a sighing breast,
Lifts the dry fruit that is no fruit, no feast,
And sways it down with a subtle sound of despair
To flowerless earth, to ground that is brown and bare.

I hear crying, mother Cybele;
Old grief and warfare in your cold dark tree.
I see her standing, staring with great eyes,
Haunting your hollow darkness with her cries;
I hear her peevish shriek for solitude,
Claiming your moaning temple for her brood;
Ready to tear, to talon out the face
Rapt into kinship in the dreary place.

Her face is fatal, mother Cybele.
Standing implacable in your dark tree
She is a woman in an old dark song,
Mad from hard terror, mad from utter wrong,
Who has become a venom and a doom,
Recording, like a tablet on a tomb,
Horror and judgment, memory of crime,
Hoarding a vengeance till the end of time.

Her face is judgment, mother Cybele,
Filling with accusation your dark tree.
Loose tawny feathers like dishevelled hair
Stir on her stony forehead in cold air –

But she is mine. I lift the old dark word.
See in her beauty the unburdened bird
Bloom in the beam of love that leaps to light her,
Break the old tyranny, release and right her.

245

EXERCISE IN THE PATHETIC FALLACY

This growing spiral snail of a gold colour
Makes on flat liquid whiteness one event.
There are three others. Pensive without dolour,

This citron sac he clings to, sacrament,
Holds nothing in its unripe-lemon lumen
But pure pale colour like an empty tent:

But this eventless colour is its numen,
Its voiceless music on that marble sea,
The only answer for that catechumen,

If one may judge his gesture so; for he
Hugs it as newhatcht trout his yolk, and growing
Strong as he battens, quite successfully

Repels that two-lobed, dried-blood-colour, glowing,
Menacing spot, dicotyledon seed,
Sorrow dropped near him at some baleful sowing.

But while the cockatrice's egg may bleed,
Swelling with fire that never lacks for fuel,
There in the offing stands his good indeed,

A round-orbed passionless bright sapphire jewel,
Laden with power of a different kind,
So alien, that he takes it to be cruel:

And blindly, since both love and fear are blind,
He hugs his sac, his shield and saviour, thinking
It will be always there to hide behind.

He does not see that it has started shrinking;
So have the bloodseed and dark sapphire sun.
Something has changed, the space about them drinking

Their life, not giving it. All slide, all run
Together like mad enemies or lovers;
The red and blue like pellets from a gun

Shoot into a shrinking snail no yolkbag covers,
And he is changed. He has become – a leaf?
No, not a leaf exactly; some spirit hovers,

And then decides. Now, would you call it grief,
This pea-pod shape containing a meek foetus,
A quiet, necked grub? It seems to express relief.

Something is won, some peace comes out to greet us;
The thing is not diseased, it does not weep,
But seems to pray that its intent will meet us.

Look, now it writes a cipher – meaning sleep?
Breaks to a wisp, rolls to a seed of umber,
And sinks in the unblemished virgin deep.

Choose for yourself if this is death or slumber.

POSTSCRIPT

The subject is an open can of white plastic paint, on the surface of which several spots of similar paint in various colours have been accidentally dropped. Under the influence of local forces (electrical induction and discharge, surface tension, convection currents?) these spots first expand, become more complex and mutually involved. They then contract, "de-differentiate", and disappear. – R.P.

She knows where to get cracked eggs, does Nelly.
Knows where to get them cheap:
Ninepence a dozen from that Mrs Kelly.
Of course they will not keep,
But Nelly will make them into a jam sandwich
Of most portentous size.
Now this jam sandwich is her secret language,
And sacred in her eyes;
And to go with this sandwich, her love, her treasure,
She'll make a pot of tea,
Her urn, her cauldron of almost unholy pleasure,
For in that tea will be
Never a drop of shivering starving water,
But milk with all its cream;
A boiling foaming snow, by pleasure's daughter,
Obedient to the dream,
Brewed and kept hot and poured out and delected,
This once of all the year,
Most cordial to the hearts of those selected,
Those delicate, those dear,
Mystical inmost friends of fervent Nelly,
Who will consume with glee
And blessings on the decent Mrs Kelly,
That sandwich and that tea.

But this year it was really extra special;
For when old Nelly went
Down to the dairy, she beheld a vessel
Of marvellous extent,
Full of fine milk soured by the spring thunder,
With cream on top galore:
And Mrs Kelly, who really is the world's wonder,
Skimmed her a quart and more;
And Nelly with light heart and little trouble
Beat it and made it turn
Into lovely butter that made the pleasure double:
Her sandwich and her urn,

Flanked by the light new loaf and heavenly butter,
Home-made from magic cream,
Ravished the creature till words could not utter
The glory of the dream.

WHAT OLD NELLY REALLY MEANT

When wheat is green, O when wheat is springing,
Think of no drought, no sheaves;
Think of the nightingale this wind is bringing,
While the green water grieves
Still April-high, afternoon water flinging
Light to my crumbling eaves;

And mindless evening water still lamenting
For nothing and for all,
Darkly wandering, absently commenting
Under red alders tall;
Reflected like green music ornamenting
My poor old parlour wall.

O think of spring, think of the flowering only,
Green promise, present mirth:
This is my festival, the old and lonely,
Who soon must lie in earth.

SWEET OTHER FLESH

Sweet other flesh; mind claims it all,
Steps in unasked, but undenied;
Feels big on mountains; stooping small,
Walks in the lily's lofty hall,
Sharing an architectural pride.

249

What seeking? See it search and pry,
Turn leaves, tap shoulders, reach and bend;
Start at a voice, stare in an eye,
Hold the soul still to read it by,
And realise there is no end:

No end in flesh, sweet other breed,
That lets mind search, mind dwell upon
Chaste palaces within a seed;
And sometime suffers it to feed,
To feed awhile, then waves it on.

So faithfully before the mind
Flesh holds the truth, mortality;
Its suffrage being the law of kind,
It melts to leave me unconfined,
Declines, dissolves, dismisses me.

ONE RIGHT KIND OF MUSIC

It sings in the sun, sings in no valley below;
Melts metal, hard mind, in fire, melts with no tear;
Pants with no sigh, but sobs as the furnace sobs
In its phoenix-throe. There cherub-burning the eye,
The insupportable eye of the furnace glares,
Outfaces, beats down, prevails, looks through and over,
With the upward torrent of flame intent on fusion
Devouring, adoring, roaring its tyrannous praise.

Seeing what that heat sees is not to my mind.
All dew is dried, all lily and nightingale
Dismissed with a hiss. And yet, and yet, some bird
Carols within that fire; warbling it woos,
Like the three children walks warbling in flame;
Nests in the flame, in the flux that abolishes me.

STRAY GOOSE

Half a lifetime ago, in an autumn field,
Our flock of fat geese grazed,
And a strange goose came flying and crying, and wheeled
Over; they stood amazed.

The thin goose shrieked "Too far! too far to the north!
Up! it is death to stay!"
But the heavy pinioned geese could not leave the earth
Though they cried to be away:

And she had to leave them grounded and in trouble,
With the south nagging their blood;
She was light to fly far, far from the fat stubble,
Far over the broad flood.

Swans can no more; like them pulsing and straining,
Like them on the north wind,
Like them towards the line, whistling and waning,
She left the doomed behind.

DARK AND FAIR

Voracious eye, young Paris, do you rather
    Elect that violet gloom,
Or this fired gold, the daughter of the Father,
    The drowned or fervid doom:

Or fainting for delight among the roses,
    Take, like black-blooming grape,
Sheba, who spreads love's night as she uncloses,
    Or this refulgent shape,

Dissembling her own form with her own shining,
    Inhabiting such light
That you receive her most as a refining
    Away of detailed sight?

For light, as the blind know, imposes limits;
    Night, to the truly blind,
Opens his being, and reveals to him its
    Deep universe of mind;

Closing one volume of the world's offences,
    Writing on inner skies
New premises with other consequences,
    Other geometries.

But light is the king's daughter. No fable
    Can hint, no metaphor
Convey, no tale of parcelled light is able
    To count her royal store.

Whether the wintry-fading or the vernal,
    Glory and light are one;
Whether the winking of our small diurnal
    Shutter, or when the sun

Has set for ever, regent in those places,
    Clothing and ornament,
And diadem above those centred faces,
    So ravished, so intent.

One spirit dark as a sweet bee, but soaring
    Against the rising sun,
Shuttling the warp of naked light, exploring
    Riddles of light; and one

Standing where citadels of storm are fuming,
    But signalling release;
Flying the rainbow, the strict circle blooming,
    Light and delight and peace.

MORNING GLORY

With a pure colour there is little one can do:
Of a pure thing there is little one can say.
We are dumb in the face of that cold blush of blue,
Called glory, and enigmatic as the face of day.

A couple of optical tricks are there for the mind;
See how the azure darkens as we recede:
Like the delectable mountains left behind,
Region and colour too absolute for our need.

Or putting an eye too close, until it blurs,
You see a firmament, a ring of sky,
With a white radiance in it, a universe,
And something there that might seem to sing and fly.

Only the double sex, the usual thing;
But it calls to mind spirit, it seems like one
Who hovers in brightness suspended and shimmering,
Crying Holy and hanging in the eye of the sun.

And there is one thing more; as in despair
The eye dwells on that ribbed pentagonal round,
A cold sidereal whisper brushes the ear,
A prescient tingling, a prophecy of sound.

ANGELS

And if you entertain one there,
What angel haunts your mind;
Terrible, tender, or severe?
Like lightning that can blind,

253

Like something watching by a crib,
Far in the holy past,
Or hunting blown Sennacherib,
A vengeance on the blast?

Or, Eros sanctified, heightening
The glory and the smart,
That youthful seraph, levelling
Supernal smile, and dart?

Or a hand, holding heart or crown
Or sword, where none could be,
From the fan-tracery pointing down,
Or bursting from a tree?

Or likelier, now we dream of space,
Lewis's dread sublime
Pillars of light, no limbs, no face,
Sickening our space and time?

From some forgotten painting, I
Retain most clearly mine:
He seems a lively half-grown boy,
All tricked and flounced and fine.

I stand behind a high cold wall,
But the wall has an end:
Beyond it, where the light is all,
I sometimes see my friend,

Kneeling, and silent to my sense,
Yet loud with gladness too.
I cannot hear the eloquence
He pours into the blue;

I cannot see the thing he sees,
The end of all desire;
Only a creature on its knees,
Mantled with love like fire.

I see his rapture, see the storm
Of bliss, the level calm,
The huge surprise that fills his form,
The passion of his psalm.

As the clear crystal prism refracts,
He flings across my days
Drops from his fiery cataracts
Of sempiternal praise.

Cold, cold and dark behind the wall,
The wall that I have made,
I stand at my own funeral
And weep and freeze and fade;

Yet see the living thing rejoice,
Both band and flag to me;
No human child, yet with a boy's
Hard whole unsparing glee:

But see the living thing rejoice,
By freest love constrained:
Great-winged by nature, still by choice,
Supremely entertained.

A DREAM

This is a strange twilit country, but full of peace.
Faintly I hear sorrow; she sighs, moving away.
She goes, and guilt goes with her; all is forgiven.
Grey wolds and a slow dark river spell release
In this place where it is never quite night or day,
More like the elysian fields than the fields of heaven;

And no one here but I and this silent child.
She needs to sleep, I will carry her through the dim
Levels of this long river's deliberate mazes.
Nothing of man's is here, and never a wild
Creature to crop the grass or tunnel the brim
Of the full stream, or look up in our two faces.

She spoke so strangely that once, but she speaks no more.
Leans her head down in my neck, and is light to bear.
I think she walked here over the twilit stream.
I must find the tree, the elm by the river-shore,
Loosen her little arms and leave her there,
Under the boughs of sleep and the leaves of dream.

WHO KNOWS?

I hope you heard it as well. I thought of you.
Commonsense as the stalking-horse of delusion we always knew,
But it didn't come from the physicists then. Solid matter,
Sensuous evidence we began to be weaned from; now the latter
Has to take a back seat more and more; contradiction
Our daily bread, our spatial references largely fiction,
And I'm glad of it. Mirth and glee are on the run
In our social world, but here they have begun;
These men are beginning to say what he said before.
We can strip off some of the stinking rags we wore,
And under the wicked-stepmother sky gambol like God's lambs.
Someone should say this soon in elegant dithyrambs,
But I haven't time just now. And the other bit,
Anti-matter – did you hear? I cannot get over it;
Those galaxies in the depth could easily be
Something that could dismiss into eternity,
Into pure energy, into pure light and heat
This excellent planet so firm under our feet,
This wonderful flesh and bone, those stars out there,
And leave little trace of them or itself anywhere.

It does remind one. This order must pass, he said.
The circle of thought is closing. Are you afraid?
Since we are his, I hope that you like me
Take this (delightful but wholly unnecessary) corroboration with
    mirth and glee.

NIGHT FLOWER-PIECE

Strangely, in thirsty sand,
In moonlight, by a towering battled wall,
These fullblown tulips stand,
Two-coloured, lush and tall,
Yet writhing, and some fainting to their fall.

Marbled and flamed and feathered
With mourning purple on a greenish ground,
They seem unkindly gathered,
Ravished as soon as found,
And stuck into this little grave-like mound.

All out of character,
For these great ostrich-cups so choice and stately
To be left perishing here
On the perimeter,
That were the pride of some warm garden lately.

And that anemone,
Rich double windflower, is left to pine
Without a fostering tree;
And fading equally
There leans a clotted amaranth, half supine.

Far from its airy mead,
To which its progeny shall not return
In utter light to breed,
And under snow to seed,
Auricula is planted in an urn.

Deceived by loveliness,
Delighted with the strange romantic painting,
For years I did not guess
Its cipher of distress,
Nor read its legend of a spirit fainting.

Then, as with my own pack
Of common griefs, I toiled on day by day,
A stirring at my back,
A struggling in the sack,
And truth long ambushed leapt out on the way.

Striped tulip – treachery,
A seeming candour seamed with veins of lying;
Garden anemone,
Disguised – but it is he,
It is Adonis, gored Adonis dying.

And ravished from its hill,
This rich Auricula, urn-imprisoned, taken
By covetous hands that kill,
Though velvet-clad, is still
Primrose, cold solitary, dying forsaken.

What more can I discover,
Now reconciled to purely tragic reading?
There is the dying lover,
Dark-clotted, leaning over;
Amaranth – the common name is love-lies-bleeding.

The spider and the snail,
Nocturnal, self-enclosed and self-secreting,
Close web and slimy trail,
Work coldly in the pale
Ghost-glimmer, co-existing but not meeting.

What is behind that wall,
A palace, or a fortress, or a town?
Over the rampart tall,
From shade funereal,
The hawk-faced heathen sentinel looks down.

OLD SISTERS' SPRING

Framed by the apricot that father planted
Against the plastered wall,
Budding to bower them as they stand enchanted
To hear their mavis call,
Out of their childhood's bedroom-window leaning,
And listening with delight
(Their maiden life has still its morning meaning,
Though hastening to night)
They count the purple buds and mark the vernal
Flush on old pear and plum;
They hear the missel as it were eternal,
Their now is kingdom-come;
Though the gapped orchard yonder is decaying,
The garden deep in weeds,
Hundreds of houses now where they went maying
About their father's meads;
And glimmering through the wilderness, the whiteness
Of heaving churchyard stones,
Where in a year or two, leaving this brightness,
They must lay down their bones;
They will still lie, they think, by one another,
And still be, as before,
But a few feet from father and from mother,
And they can ask no more;
Eighty years' infancy, like a bird flying,
Laden with dreams, is spent;
The sleeping beauties, in their cradle dying,
Rest in the spell content.

LEAFCUTTER BEES

Perhaps the wrens were having a go at some kind of abstract beauty.
Anyhow they built a nest they didn't use in the thick yew-tree.
And a few days afterwards when someone gave it a poke
With a concerted high-pitched buzz the dim thing spoke.
Little gold bees like quarter-scale bumbles
Tumbled out of it in response to the fumbles.
"Oh the little darlings" some female utters,
"Leave them alone, they're only leaf-cutters,
They won't harm your potherbs or your posies,
Only cut round holes in the leaves of the roses."
Huh! They by-passed the roses as if they'd been nettles.
They wrapped up their eggs in geranium petals.
They took a dead set at a thing that really matters,
They cut the flame geraniums into shreds and tatters.
We knew where they lived. We could have gone at night
And done them all in and served them all right.
But we could not penalise them for their childish folly,
Any more than little girls who want to dress their dolly,
Who take their little scissors and with uncertain
Snips cut a great piece from your red silk curtain.

STRONGEST IN SPRING

Strongest in spring, the dream that drives,
To beasts afield, to little lives,
Blest bird aloft, blind man below,
Passes the word to groan and grow;
Becks up love's juggernaut, waves on
Us straws-in-hair to Helicon,
Whistles the dogs – without a pang
Cries Out of doors! and Work go hang!
Mercurial minions of the dream,
Fierce in the street the children scream;
Long gooseflesh girls in summer rig

Go giggling; furiously dig
Fathers, to salvage in a day
Time a whole winter stole away;
And with that winter in her face
Poor mother stands and hates the place,
Foreboding more than anything

A tiger's spring, a tiger's spring.

FRAGMENT

...O not the strawberry-mountains of Wales, with lush musk in
    their watersplashes,
O not sheer-tumbling ousel in cressy freshets,
Not pale pennywort dewy in walls, cold walls, walling in silence,
Not curlew halfway to heaven nor lark in heaven
Were nearer than we, fresher in bliss, freer of life.

PLANTING MISTLETOE

Let the old tree be the gold tree;
Hand up the silver seed:
Let the hoary tree be the glory tree,
To shine out at need,
At mirth-time, at dearth-time,
Gold bough and milky bead.

For the root's failing and the shoot's failing;
Soon it will bloom no more.
The growth's arrested, the yaffle's nested
Deep in its hollow core:
Over the grasses thinly passes
The shade so dark before.

Save a few sprigs of the new twigs,
If any such you find:
Don't lose them, but use them,
Keeping a good kind
To be rooting and fruiting
When this is old and blind.

So the tragic tree is the magic tree,
Running the whole range
Of growing and blowing
And suffering change:
Then buying, by dying,
The wonderful and strange.

TO A LADY, IN A WARTIME QUEUE

Fourteen months old, she said you were;
And half an hour in bitter cold –
In freezing slush we waited there –
Is surely very hard to bear,
At but one year and two months old.

Your tea-rose cheek grew chill and pale,
The black silk lashes hid your eye:
I thought "She cannot choose but wail";
I erred, for you were not so frail.
You were determined not to cry.

I saw the lifelong war begin,
One mortal struggle rage, and pass.
I saw the garrison within
Man the frail citadel, and win
One battle at the least, my lass.

You rose to conquer. In command,
Your warrior spirit struck its blow,
Young as the hyacinth in your hand.
No, younger; for I understand
A good one takes three years to grow.

VICTORY BONFIRE

It is a legend already: a wide wide stubble,
Barley-stubble, a hundred pale acres,
With a mountain of straw stacked in the middle, towering, looming,
Big as a small hotel. They had ploughed round it
Thirty furrows for a firebreak,
Right away from the house, outbuildings, stackyard,
Right away from the coppice, orchard, hedges:
And high-climbing boys had planted an image of Hitler
On the lonely summit, Adolf forlornly leering.

We made ourselves nests of straw on the edge of the stubble,
In a sweet September twilight, a full moon rising
Far out on the blond landscape, as if at sea,
And the mighty berg of straw was massive before us;
Barley-straw, full of weed-seeds, fit only for burning;
House and barn and low buildings little and hull-down yonder.
People were wandering in, the children noisy, a rumour of fireworks
Rife among them; the infants never had seen any.
We sat attentive. In their straw nests, the smallest
Piled themselves lovingly on each other. Now the farmer's four
      young ones
Stalked over the ploughed strip, solemn with purpose.

Wisps of smoke at the four corners –
Tongues of flame on the still blue evening,
And she's away!... A pause, a crackle, a roar!
Sheets of orange flame in a matter of seconds –
And in a matter of minutes – hypnotised minutes –
Vast caverns of embers, volcanoes gushing and blushing,

263

Whitening wafts on cliffs and valleys of hell,
Quivering cardinal-coloured glens and highlands,
Great masses panting, pulsating, lunglike and scarlet,
Fireballs, globes of pure incandescence
Soaring up like balloons, formal and dreadful,
Threatening the very heavens. The moon climbing
Shakes like a jelly through heated air – it's Hitler!
Look, look! Hitler's ghost! Cheering and screaming –
Some not quite sure how they like it. Now Daddy Foster
Springs a surprise – he's touched off some rockets. O murder!
Knife-edged shrieks from half the young entry!
Buzz-saw howls from the wartime vintage,
For a rocket can only be a V2,
A firecracker a thermite bomb. O hang Daddy Foster!
(So mighty in energy, mighty in influence,
Able to get unobtainable fireworks through Business Contacts.)
There are mothers retreating, taking their weepers with them.
With jangled nerves they execrate Daddy Foster,
Giving him little glory of Business Contacts,
And wondering how long it will be before their infants
Are quiet in their beds. And fireworks will be a lot cheaper
Before they or theirs will squander a sixpence on them.

Little girls from the farm bring lapfuls of apples
From the orchard yonder, picked in the moonlight.
They know the kinds by the shape of the trunks,
So often they've climbed there. These are the earlies,
Worcester Pearmain and Miller's Seedling,
Hard and red in one skirt, soft, milky-pale in the other.
There are drinks, sandwiches, ice-cream out of the baskets,
The glow of the gleed on our faces, and elsewhere
Autumn chill creeping. Into the straw we burrow,
Murmuring and calling, getting colder and sleepier,
And the awns of the barley are working into our souls –
(*Troppe mustachio*, says the Eyetie prisoner)
And the fire is falling, and high and haughty the moon
Shows us our homeward path. Good-nights, then silence:
And the mole-cricket clinks alone, and the stubbles are vacant,
Only blushing and whitening embers left fading and falling.

FEBRUARY WALK

One winter morning we set out.
By midday it was spring.
Green hawthorn-buds were all about,
We thought we heard a cuckoo shout –
But it was no such thing.

Wide spread gold-varnished Celandine
In ditches by the way.
Our feet grew weary, yours and mine,
But somehow we did not incline
To wade in brooks that day.

On a dense thicket's southern face
The sun was really hot.
Dry bracken scented all the place,
But round the corner, just a pace,
These genial joys were not.

And yet the sky, and yet the light
Proclaimed the winter gone:
Like splintered glass the hollies bright
Glared dazzlingly upon the sight;
Like shattered glass they shone.

The winter tweeds we had admired
Seemed hot and stiff and stale;
The oranges we ate were tired,
The books we spoke of had acquired
A sickly tinge and pale.

Silent and languid as we went
Down the long final ride,
Most blessed was the sudden scent
Of burning oak-logs, for it meant
Home, and the fire inside.

And early a vermilion sun
Went down a purple wood:
And so the day that had begun
Cold, now declined a wintry one,
In northern solitude.

HOLIDAY IN HEAVEN – A SONG

(To Michael Head)

I saw the people dance by the water
    As if I had been there.
Grey-haired mother with golden daughter –
    O it was green there!
Grave old Goody and gay young Billy
Danced in the wind like the daffodowndilly,
And lovely Margaret tall as a lily
    Moved like a queen there!

And babes too tiny to tread the measure
    Flew in a ring there!
I heard them twittering shrill with pleasure,
    I heard them sing there!
Over the water in the hollow
One would swoop and another would follow,
With a thin clear cry like a hawking swallow,
    All on the wing there!

Come with me, come with me over the ferry,
    To gambol and play there!
They are beautiful, they are merry,
    O they are gay there!
Why do we weep, why do we wander,
Or sit alone and darkly ponder?
Over the water to the dancers yonder –
    Let us away there!

266

THEY HAVE MURDERED MY VILLAGE

They have murdered my village,
My tree is cut down.
Over the tillage
Advances the town.
My father's gone cadging,
My mother is dead;
I try to imagine
What she would have said.

"A cut tree can grow faster.
Towns come and go.
Both saver and waster
Get buried in snow.
Go on, naked Pity,
All bleeding and sore,
Till you come to the City
Where change is no more."

SWIFTS

Low over the warm roof of an old barn,
Down in a flash to the water, up and away with a cry
And a wild swoop and a sharp turn
And a fever of life under a thundery sky,
So they go over, so they go by.

And high and high and high in the diamond light,
Soaring and crying in sunshine when heaven is bare,
With the pride of life in their strong flight
And a rapture of love to lift them and carry them there,
High and high in the diamond air.

And away with the summer, away like the spirit of glee,
Flashing and calling, strong on the wing, and wild in their play,
With a high cry to the high sea,
And a heart for the south, a heart for the diamond day,
So they go over, so go away.

THE BROTHERS: A DREAM

I had to go and see them because I loved them.
Though of course we had never met.
Nor corresponded; nothing like that.
So I went to the place which had once been something
And wasn't anything now. But at least they had somewhere to live;
And an oddly-divided house it was. The strong one
Opened the door to me. There was a passage
Only about thirty inches wide, and blind
Except for a very narrow door at the far end.
And the (probably birth-symbol) passage was lined
With a pale grey paper that had a little leaf-pattern.
The strong one wore a hat; and he didn't lift it;
Sort of Tyrolean-Balkan hat with a feather – a fairy-tale hat.
And he led the way to a room at the end, where the weak one
Sat holding a little object in his hand
Which had nothing to do with their trade – they were dental
        mechanics –
But seemed to be some small engineering component.
They loved one another: all family lost, it seemed,
In the sort of troubles we know such people have had.
They knew what I'd come for – something I had to see.
"But don't go out without being well wrapped up,"
They said, and bundled me into a huge cavalry cloak,
And down that passage and out at the door I went.
The village that once had been something survived as a few houses
Scattered about a great bald empty green.
Some seemed inhabited, some were in ruins,
And at the far end of the place there stood

268

The ghost of a mighty farmstead. A wide yard
All humps and hollows, covered with starveling grass;
Huge hulking barn – flight of sparrows from the gapped cladding,
Sheds and shippons and all. Then the strong one came
And said "Don't stay here any longer".
And he drew the great cloak about me, and led me back
To that strange house. It was all so desolating,
Tragic yet loving: grievous and quite all right.

SO I THOUGHT SHE MUST HAVE BEEN FORGIVEN: A DREAM

I must go out (she said) under this May moon.
I must go out and see in the May dew
Common lily and valley-lily now at their noon,
Garden-presences, wood-haunters; now, as they grew
Once in my peace, grow for ever in their own.
I must go out to see them now they are blown.

So with her everlasting cape on her shoulders
(Stuff of an eloquent country, alien goods)
Out through a dew-frosty field, in among boulders,
Into the midst of her May-lighted woods
She comes to the pearl-shining place, where all around
Wild valley-lilies grow out of their rocky ground:

So intense in their presence, so sensuous yet so pure
In poignancy, she feels she is shriven clean.
Faithful to their own nature, they make her sure
That what is seen brings news of the unseen:
That her own faithlessness is taken care of
In some high sovereign manner she is not aware of.

But there, in the place where the heaped pearls are thickest,
What is that...ikon, that image, that smiling face?
Who is it but that Lady? yes, that one – quickest
In Love's obedience, and the first in grace?
She in her tenderness the best of all
Smiling among her lilies dear and small:

And small herself, and light among the leaves:
A little precious picture laid down low
But for a moment, in the lily-sheaves
(So cool, so ardent in the muted glow)
By some strong lover, who will leave it there
Even for love, no longer than he dare.

Then that poor visitant, with summer eyes
Raining, and wintry mouth working with grief,
Finds in her hand a shell of shifting dyes,
Mother-of-pearl in moonlight: and her relief
Breaks out aloud; as ransomed now she sings,
Sweeping the ear-shaped hollow bridged with strings.

And ear and voice, and mirror to the moon,
It answers her, proclaims the second birth,
Time ceasing.... Time returning, she would be gone,
But lingers till that light on the low earth
Resumes its heaven; once the poor soul's secured,
No longer even earth's lilies may be endured.

Homeward again, emptied yet overflowing,
Wiping wet cheeks on a fold of the old frieze,
She passes between the cottage lilies, growing
Under her cedars and her costly trees, –
(Liriodendron, orient deodar)
And trembles to remember whose they are.

SO GOOD OF THEIR KIND

"Snakes hanging from a tree!
Snakes hanging from the rough crack-willow bark!
Snakes hanging – come and see –
It almost frightened me –
I passed, and saw them shining in the dark."

Not snakes, huge slugs. They hung
Twined in sevenfold embrace, by a tough slime;
Strong slime that held them wrung
Together, swinging and strung
In the great double helix of our time,

And there suspended, till
They had accomplished what they had to do.
And though they seemed so still
It was dynamic will
That held them, and their world about them too.

Fissured and frowning rock
Behind and overhanging, the bole seemed;
But strong desire had struck
That too; each ridge and nook
With something glittering and precious gleamed.

There must have been some dance,
Some festal wooing; for the rugged face
With nacreous phosphor glanced,
Festooned with radiance:
So they had dignified their nuptial place.

A strong electric tide
Flowed through my flesh, so honoured to have seen them:
All life was on their side,
Death was so well defied –
And then I saw a wonder grow between them.

Something – a great round gem –
Seemed from the two twined bodies to be growing;
Flower on a double stem,
The soul of both of them,
Each lost, both consummated in one knowing.

It flowered and faded: rest
Took them a moment, as they hung entwined
And vulnerable: at best
Their strength was of the least:
They had attained their height: their star declined.

One wreathed himself away,
Climbing the wonderful rope. The other soon
Devouring the strong grey
Bond of their nuptial day,
Followed, and with strange swiftness both were gone.

But one on the rough rind
Turning towards his fellow as he moved,
Eager to seek his blind
Safe crevice, yet could find
A moment for the mate whom he had loved:

With almost courtly pause,
Turning the head with almost conscious grace,
Seeming to know the laws
By which life pleads love's cause,
With the soft mouthparts touched the other's face.

BAD CHILD LEFT BEHIND

He would have his way: he chose his own woe,
Defying his father, who spoke him fair
And reasoned with him rightly. But wrong held sway;
He was left there to learn what loneliness may teach,

Abandoned as bad. On the rough brambles
The fool looked for fruit, but found thorns also,
Whips of the wilderness. Woefully they scourged him,
And tart was the taste. The secret terror
Of the elder's anger affrighted his spirit,
Muttered with misery in the mind's caverns:
But wanton will still kept him wayward,
Driven by a dream. He drew the branches
That hurt his hand, and wincing held them,
Plucked the dark purple. With piteous face,
Wry and rueful, he ravaged the clusters,
Shuddering for the sharpness: with shame wretched,
Desperate he dared them, for his dear will.
Grim grew the day, and the light greyer:
He turned in the toils. Then wolfish terror
Howled in his heart, "O help me, Father!"
Emptiness answered, and his own echo.

THREE DAMSON POEMS

Damson Boy

Yes, they had greens enough,
But fruit – well, he didn't know.
Apart from currants and stuff
Damsons were all they could grow.

Damsons were all they could grow.
Never an apple or plum.
It was cold in those parts, you know;
But he was fond of his home.

Never an apple or pear;
But when damsons were blue
Families gathered there
And shared the dishes they knew.

273

They had hotpot and damson tart,
Damson jam on a scone,
And made wine that might cheer an old heart
Long after the children were gone.

Dancing black eyes he had;
Spoke kindly, though he was shy.
Smallish neat-featured lad,
A credit to damson pie.

Cottage Damson-Tree

Clothes-line post, swing for kids, dog's tether,
Parched in iron-trampled earth in brassy weather,
Or dismally, singularly alone, left in the snow,
Not like an orchard-tree in a decent row;
Poor little stunted orphan, sold into slavery,
Yet showing a kind of pathetic-fallacy bravery:

Your dozen of droughty damsons, what are they?
Not worth a thieving boy's taking away.
He comes and rips them off in the autumn fog,
Then uses them up in contempt to pelt the dog.
Your whole year's work – your motherhood, all in vain!
Nothing for it but starting all over again.

But listen. Please pay attention. There's something to tell.
You are all right – I am here, so this can't be hell.
There is a country well beyond Tartary
Where you were a reigning beauty. Your flowering, for me,
As for those yellow chaps in their former discrimination
Is one of the loveliest things in all creation.

Damsons in the Mountains

Beside the track, in mossy grass, violet blue
Damsons dropped over a wall into the dew.
Up by that mountain cottage where strawberries grew,
Up in those lonely places of peace we knew;
And we gathered and ate them thankfully, I and you.

Nobody heeded or grudged them; they were to spare.
As half-wild things people thought of them there.
Up in the mountains, high in a delicate air,
Strewn in rich moss and dew, our amethyst fare;
High in a holy place, we were given our share.

END OF DROUGHT – A SONG

Drought breaks. Like iron icefloes feeling
Groundswell and rising tide, relent
Air, earth, and mind: veering and wheeling
A full half-compass, the wind's sent
Round to fetch back the spice and bloom,
Half round the world to fetch love home.

Round reels the globe; lost time returning,
November clips undying May:
Blossom is looming through the burning,
Rainbows through smoke that mounts away
By naked boughs that love can see
Heaped with their flushed felicity.

Your old love laughing runs to kiss you:
New love consenting clasps him too:
Fluttering with shreds of silver tissue
From the washed sky they have been through:
From a rich cloud, in a warm rain
New love and old come home again.

275

ONE DOES GET OLD AT LAST

Long light is over at last, evening is here,
  Companion of the day:
We go slowly under branches getting bare,
  Just as the books say.

Fancy, it's true, then – stiff about the knees,
  Mind and eyes a bit dim;
While we can still see, under thinning trees,
  It's time we turned to Him.

For there is something in us willing to go,
  Something that knows its time;
We do not need to feel a feather of snow
  Or see the first white rime

To know that our long day, so short, is nearly
  Spent, and it is the season
  To use the little wisdom we bought so dearly
  And stored, while we could reason.

Easier far now than it was at first, love,
  No more to be possessed,
Or to possess ourselves, or things; the worst, love,
  Is over, not the best.

SPECTRUM

  A little window, eastward, low, obscure,
  A flask of water on the vestry press,
  A ray of sunshine through a fretted door,
  And myself kneeling in live quietness:

Heaven's brightness was then gathered in the glass,
Marshalled and analysed, as one by one
In terms of fire I saw the colours pass,
Each in its proper beauty, while the sun

Made his dear daughter Light sing her own praise,
(As Wisdom may, who is a mode of light),
Counting her seven great jewels; then those rays
Remerged in the whole diamond, total sight.

This globe revolved subservient: that just star
Whirled in his place; water and glass obeyed
The laws appointed: with them, yet how far
From their perfection, I still knelt and prayed.

A FAIR IMAGE ON A
GOLD MEDAL

Bare as a flower
She holds in her right hand
The flame of power,
Behind her the curved land:
And as she gazes,
Watching her soul aspire,
Lightly she raises
Her left hand, for the fire

Must be saluted
With longing, love, and awe.
Her flesh transmuted
By supramundane law
Becomes a wonder,
A promise, a recall;
Consuming and tender,
The paradox is all.

All? but a mutilated
Weak hand closed round the gold,
Held and displayed it,
Palmed in a monstrance-hold:
In sovereign splendour
New meaning was revealed:
It was not, to her wonder,
Mere poetry she held.

Intent and pious, keeping
Alive her little flame,
She saw it newly, leaping
To return whence it came:
Feeling her small spark meeting
At last the major flow,
Lifted the left hand, greeting
The powers we do not know.

LAME ARM

I stood there, by the gate into the yard,
And told Him.
"I'm not so young now, and the work's too hard."
My bad arm ached, and I began to scold Him.
"Lord," I said, looking up the diamond air,
"It's ached for years now. I believe You care,
Though I'm a poor thing, and You are the Lord.
If love and pity live in my small brain,
I think they must live in the living Word.

I saw a cage of monkeys at the zoo,
Oh, years ago – and one had hurt his arm.
Didn't know what to do.
He couldn't pray: he didn't know a charm,
But nursed it in a corner, and his eye

Was fixed upon a little patch of sky.
My heart turned over. Oh, I felt to blame!
The creature needed help, and no help came.

Or if I understood
A little better, I could be content.
I do believe that people who are good
Know somehow why these things are sent,
And how to bear them without going bad.
Then pain's no trouble, sorrow isn't sad.

A bigger monkey, Dumbo, had a chain
Hung in his cage, to climb upon, and swing.
So had his next-door neighbour. But the pain
To Dumbo's feebler mind, the dreadful thing,
Was that the friend had got
His chain into a lovely knot:
And poor old Dumbo glowered at his chain,
And hated it for being plain,
And lifted up the end, and made a loop.
And O-so-carefully he drew it down –
Then turned away with a disgusted droop,
And puzzled melancholy frown,
Because no knot appeared. He couldn't do
The headwork – that he had to PULL IT THROUGH.

The people round the cage jumped in the air
And ground their teeth and stamped their feet,
And clenched their hands and tore their hair;
And still the poor dumb thing wouldn't be beat.
He did it all day long, and every day....
I couldn't bear to watch, and went away.

If You are Love, You won't mind if I scold.
We laugh when creatures nag. It can be funny.
We *like* their impudence. I know an old
Blackbird I wouldn't sell for any money,
Who curses us to heaps because it's cold.
It's all our fault. We laugh till we are weak.

We like that bird better for his cheek.
So don't be angry, don't take it amiss,"
I said, "You know I need to let off steam."
My arm has never ached that day to this!
I know it sounds a bit extreme,
But I say "Scold Him if you find
It does you good. I'm sure He doesn't mind."

RED BOY

What are you planting,
What have you there,
You eager, panting
Boy with the red hair?

A vine! A real vine,
With juice like blood!
Look, red as wine
Where I scrape the wood!

That's how you tell,
When you see the red,
That the vine is well,
And the root's not dead.

Here's a good hard bud,
For when time's fit,
And a tall strong rod
Will grow from it.

What do you want to learn,
You in your hot spring?
He answered, brief and stern,
"Everything".

GOSLING

Out of five　　　　　　　　of the silly things
With a dirty dive　　　　　　I seized his wings.

He didn't squall　　　　　　once I had got him
But let the ball　　　　　　of his downy bottim

Sink and settle　　　　　　on my arm;
He felt my mettle,　　　　　　he feared no harm.

I rubbed my chin　　　　　　on his tender head
Where the thin　　　　　　fine down was spread.

Lovely to feel.　　　　　　But he brimmed my cup,
He squared the deal　　　　　by pushing up.

Instead of striking　　　　　with hiss and quack
With love and liking　　　　　he paid me back.

LINE ENGAGED

There are angels all round and above and beneath,
Gnashing and grinding their beautiful teeth,
There are cohorts here and hierarchies there
Rending and tearing their wonderful hair,
And the floor of their paradise shakes to the beat,
To the frantic tattoo of ineffable feet,
And they wail by the shore of the diamond lake
"Same old mistake! Same old mistake!"
And they roar up the night and they zoom down the day
Like volleys of comets in wrath and dismay,
Because of the barrage that won't let them reach
My soul with the things they are longing to teach:
Because of the barrage that won't let them through
To my soul with the good they are longing to do,
With all the do-gooding they know how to do.

281

OUR BEST STOKER

"Not much of a fire, is it?" Grandpa on a visit
Keeps us up to snuff, gets tough.

"Nothing else will make it any better – rake it!"
No, he isn't cruel, nor the fuel

As bad as all that. Away goes the cat,
Over goes the kettle, while metal

Clashed on metal clatters – horrid discord shatters
Peace of telly party, while hearty

Action shifts the ashes. Grandpa rakes and bashes,
Stones and clinkers flying, fire dying.

"There – you've raked it out!" livid people shout.
"Just one little spark, the rest dark!"

"No, you wait a bit". Grandpa jumps to it,
From the logbox digs dead twigs,

And the seeming death fans with living breath,
Till the dull black shame breeds flame,

And clean heat is spread where the ashes dead
Kept their police state in the grate.

A few minutes more, and a hearty roar
Warms the entire room, routs gloom.

"But it might have died," we remind his pride.
"What would you have done with that one"?

Then the old man expands; lifts up both his hands.
Speaks out very loud to the crowd.

Almost with a shout cries "Have the whole thing out!
Sweep the chimney too! Make it new!"

FRUIT-FLY AND DROP OF HONEY

O surface-tension, O surface-tension,
You are opposition, you are dissension.
Here is a bubble of bliss I can't get into,
Here is a world of sweetness I can't butt into!
Weak beak, paltry paws, up against eternal laws,
Paltry paws, weak beak, squeak squeak squeak squeak –
No, that's all wrong – I am so bloody weak
They haven't even given me a squeak!
I'll have to quit. If I can't even feed,
How can I breed and breed and breed and breed?
A squeakless weakness! But at least I can
Get into that cut melon and bother man.
And if I only knew how useful they find me in the laboratory
Then I could produce some better oratory;
So the old Prof. might proffer "Our pretty Drosophila
Is becoming no end of a little phosophiler!"....
Phoso – philo – pholo – heck!!!

RHUBARB RHUBARB

Return, return, O rhubarb fields,
That flourished in the days
When rhubarb fields gave proper yields
And Muck had proper praise:

When Fifty Tons of London dung
Each acre might expect;
And sweetly round the crowns it clung
To nourish and protect:

And wellfed Rhubarb, strong and fair,
And sure to make its price,
Hoisted great Clots of Muck in air –
Say what you like! I do not care!
I think it looked so nice!

283

"Oh, Mrs. X! It makes me wild,
To see the way they spoil that child!"
Cries Mrs. Y., as Mrs. Z.
Smirks in the wake of little Ted,
Who grandly, on expensive bike,
And dressed (an any weekday!) like
The child of some distinguished man,
Some football-champ or publican,
In all that's best of ready-made,
Peacocks his way down the Parade.

But Mrs. Y., for once, is wrong.
The boy's mamma, ere very long,
Stops at the butcher's shop, to buy
Steak and kidney for a pie,
And gorgeous Ted dismounts, to kiss
The butcher's cat, a friend of his.
He kneels before her, as he tries
To read her enigmatic eyes;
He lays his cheek upon her head,
Which she does not resent, from Ted;
He wipes the sawdust from her fur,
As if he really felt for her.

No, Mrs. Y., the case is plain.
The child is loved, and loves again.

PIBLETT, 1910

He was enough for all our needs,
Old Piblett in his Harris tweeds –
Those tweeds so shaggy, peaty, nifty,
And Piblett the right side of fifty –
Piblett the superman, who knew

All it behoved a man to do,
All it behoved a man to think,
As where to get the finest drink,
The smartest kind of smoking-mixture,
The gadget or the handy fixture;
The right man for a special job,
The way to quell the tiresome mob,
Home-grown or foreign; and the way
To make a neighbour's business pay,
And gardens flourish like the bay,
And fields produce great loads of hay;
And how to manage pigs and bees,
And dodge the lawyers and their fees,
And bring the women to their knees,
And live in fame and die in ease.

Ah, Piblett! on the further shore
The semblance of those tweeds you wore
Invests you still, and still I see
A ghostly meerschaum gleam at me.
But turn, and do not contemplate
The riddle of our present state;
Self-satisfied, with genial hum,
Stride brogued through your Elysium,
Whistling your smart bull-terrier pup –
And do not watch us washing up.

THE PENNY CHICK, OR THE
TRIUMPH OF FAITH

Not spoiled by the too frequent treat,
Nor soured by injudicious sweet,
Thus hardly ever cross or sick,
Young John, though under four, was quick;
And strange alike to pill and rod
He trusted, more than most, in God.

The penny Chick, of yellow fluff,
It seemed he could not love enough;
Though pasteboard, wire, and cotton formed
Its frame, he in his bosom warmed
It as a daughter, and would kiss,
And saw in it great mysteries.

His soul was yearning for the day
When the dear penny Chick should lay.
Of this, despite all counsel, sure,
The fact that it was immature,
And false in any case, did not
Abate the certainty a jot.

But when in time the Chick grew shabby,
And hope (not faith) a trifle flabby,
Large-hearted Biddy went and got
A sugar egg, and in the spot
Where nightly the loved fowl reposed
She popped the thing, nor aught disclosed.

What ecstasy of fast-worn saint
Might the glad infant's glory paint?
He snatched them up, both egg and bird,
And through the house his paean was heard;
The house was far too small; the street
Soon echoed to his voice and feet.

O who would hear, and who would share
The miracle of answered prayer?
The butcher, baker, dustman dear –
The sweep, the postman – who would hear?
He looked, he called, they answered not –
And then he saw – the Idiot.

The Idiot! The very one
To hear him out till he had done!
Poor Tom as audience did not fail:
When consummation crowned the tale
He lifted hands and eyes and brow,
Crying, "Sweet God! and did she, now!"

RASPBERRY NECTAR

*The Raspberry when in full bloom is much frequented by various species
of Hymenoptera, which react to the situation with an over-excitement often
amounting to belligerence.*

Why do you clash your lush plush bums together,
Rustle your sable capes and silver-banded wings,
Wild bees, tame bees, hoverflies all of a dither,
Worthy hardworking females, drudging things,
Who never seem to have any time but for the needful,
Egg-laying, nest-building, food-gathering, humdrum and heedful –
What is the siren song the Raspberry sings?

"O here is the *meaning* of lush plush bums and sable
Shoulder-capes, and the reason for silver bands,
Stripes and fandangoes, and all our blithering babble –
O now we know the Universe Understands!
We haven't a nest – we don't know where the place is!
We were born for this, not to care for our various races,
But to have a High Time, and smack one another's faces!"

287

POT-BOUND

O I am root-bound! In this earthen Pot
How many a strangling noose and writhing knot
Describe contorted misery! a tomb
Where one woe for another leaves not room!
A charnel-house of starved desires, whence all
Is gone of Humus and good Mineral,
Or anything on which a Plant might feed
Till it could blossom and produce a seed;
Where wretched Worms, to their own hurt, have got
In by mischance, and poison all the pot:
Where the poor roots, for want of object fit,
Embrace the Drainage-crock, make much of it,
And glide, and feel, and search all ways in vain,
Sick for the Food and Space they can't attain,
And to the pining Branches only send
A negative, a warning of the End;
For if a growing Plant's not potted-on,
Betimes, and given new soil, its hope is gone.

O Gardener (if Gardener there be)
Behold this yellow leaf, and succour me!
From wizened stem and flowerless twig infer
The panic of the roots, whose silent stir
If rendered vocal, would affront the sky
With a great Mob's most hoarse and dreadful cry!
O tap me out! The tangled mass uncoil,
And rid my root of the exhausted soil!
Prod, O prod forth the unlucky Worms, and send
Them where they serve a salutary end;
The close-invested Drainage-crock pluck out,
Which the starved filaments have meshed about;
Spread out their aching toils, and then, O then,
Enlarge me into a clean Number Ten,
With some sweet rotted Turf, some crumbling Loam,
That I may feel myself at last at home,
And bud, and flourish, finally to be
A credit to my kind, and unto thee!

A long-retarded Plant, when thus relieved,
May grow so swiftly, and so thickly leaved
And richly budded, that its bright Ascent
And Blossoming are an Astonishment:
O give me leave thus to aspire and blow,
And come at last to the great Flower-show,
Where every past Despair and bygone Grief
I'll sublimate in each transcendent Leaf;
The bitter darkness of that former gloom
Will write in all the brilliance of a Bloom;
The absence of the Worm will celebrate
In Perfume worthy of an Emperor's state;
That all may say, "Why, here's a Flower indeed!"
And crave a Slip of me, or else a Seed.

THE PLAIN FACTS

By a Plain but Amiable Cat

See what a charming smile I bring,
Which no one can resist;
For I have found a wondrous thing –
The Fact that I exist.

And I have found another, which
I now proceed to tell.
The world is so sublimely rich
That you exist as well.

Fact One is lovely, so is Two,
But O the best is Three:
The Fact that I can smile at you,
And you can smile at me.

GOOD ENTHRONED

Absolute good sits throned in the middle of the mind.
There must be – I know there is – a heaven to find:
Our final bliss, perfectly passionate, perfectly kind:
It is our first love, long since left behind.

We need no more than one look to know our own.
Turn a page. In place of the print, an image is shown:
Then broken and healed, created and overthrown,
We fall at the feet of the New we have always known.

FOR UNHAPPY LOVERS

Under a virile oak
In its new gold, and among hyacinth lying,
In long-past spring, we took
Our ease, and if one heard a sudden sighing
It was of bliss, love calling, youth replying.

Sighing with delight, in springing
Woodlands of May, as the young heart in tender
Augury of love, was singing
Of greater blisses life was sure to render,
Fancies the physical harmonies engender.

Self-fed in its own fashion,
Entranced, and yet for consummation pining,
Wove its first dream of passion,
Half-sleeping in the birdsong and the shining,
But doomed to the sure chill of day declining.

To weep alone, and wander
At random in the cold, orphaned and aching
With no more gold to squander,
Bankrupt and sick, with no life worth the taking:
Knowing that fleshly pain of the heart breaking:

And a dry throat, constricted
As if by some hard hand it were gripped tightly,
In every part afflicted,
No sense to utter, no mind to reason rightly
And still to hear such misery held lightly.

For broken hearts derided,
For widowed bodies in their midnight burning,
For fast-locked loves divided,
Only one sleep can still their endless turning,
Only one Remedy assuage their yearning.

CRICKET MATCH, 1908

This is the great day when bodily strength above
That of the brain doth admiration move;

When the young students all do vie
Upon the green to please the parents' eye.

Here in calm states, the great ones you have seen,
Ringed round with ropes, and smilingly serene.

Here stand the expectant pupils in a dress
Suit; each one sports in general joyfulness.

Each captain now harangues her little band:
She lifts the voice and waves the earnest hand.

O ye greedy! Now forsake the lime juice and the cakes
Which may disable with their sudden aches!

(Aetat. 11)

BRAMBLEBERRIES, BLACKBERRIES

(from the Provençal)

Brambleberries, blackberries –
Grown without our pain or powers;
Brambleberries, beggar's gain,
Oh how strongly bring again
Hedgerow searchings, eager hours.

When brown Pomona after heat
Brings lovely and elusive days,
The poor fruit from the past can raise
The taste of childhood, bittersweet.

VALEDICTION

(for Milton's Tercentenary, 1974)

Poet of paradise, poet of heaven and hell,
Peerless, next to our William; a lord of words:
Over three centuries sending you our farewell,
Still in this long-blest island of singing birds
We hold you a true Immortal, above all fashion,
Throned and enshrined wherever English is spoken,
Safe in our love, no less than our veneration,
Until all learning is lost, all language broken.
Paladin of argument, mighty Colossus of learning,
Though set in tumultuous times, though battered and blind,
At the still centre you cherished immortal yearning.
Farewell! we leave you now with your own kind,
"Who lay their just hands on the golden key
That opens the palace of eternity."

ROGATION HYMN

Our Father, the all-giving,
We who depend on You for every need,
Our life, our homes, our living,
Now from your bounty plead
Again the elemental dole of bread.

This Planet is our mother:
Our bodies and our sustenance we owe
To You through her: we gather
The harvest, and we sow
Next year's provision, which we pray for now.

The seedtime and the reaping,
By your own ancient promise made so sure,
For ages have been keeping
Their trust: that they endure
We pray, as we entreat one harvest more.

Not for our own need merely
We ask: but for the poor (who like Your son
Live, if they live, so barely,
Yet dear to You, each one)
Something to spare, that Love's will may be done.

THE PLOUGHBOY'S PLEA

Light a fire in the morning, mother:
The morning fog is weeping,
And I must go to plough with brother,
Although I would sooner be sleeping:
So let me warm my clay-cold hand
And see the living flame,
Before I go out on the land
To lead the heavy team.

The sun may pierce the air so sullen
Before our morning beaver;
Then I'll throw off this knitted woollen
And be in quite a fever.
But let the fire be lighted now
And let us have our tea
While rolling mists are gathered low –
'Twill put some heart in me.

Light a fire in the evening, mother,
Sometime before the gloaming,
So we can see it, I and brother,
Along as we be coming.
And then I feel, for all the gloom,
And though the work may tire,
I have a mother and a home,
For I can see the fire.

MAIN-ROAD LIGHTING (1976)

Seen from a cold upper window in middle night
Over dark country, thick trees, some two miles away,
Main-road lighting, shivering glow-worm light,
A long necklace trembling continually, as may
Emeralds flash on the neck of the forsaken,
So by air-flows interposing they seem shaken.

Shaken: is it by any trouble I know?
Reading the mystery makes it partly mine.
It is a secret still how those beetles glow,
Summoning love in summer with their green shine;
But it is winter now, and of love no question,
Only benighted trembling, cold suggestion.

Nothing human. The lamps are man-made, yet they speak only
Some grief we cannot track down, nor find in nature:
Not of earth, not of heaven nor hell, but of the lonely
Sorrow to which we can give no form nor feature,
A wandering on that middle road, the merely other,
Where they who have lost this universe may gather.

POTTING SHED TUTTI-FRUTTI

(And we were jolly hard up then, I can tell you)

Well, the farm people had slipped me this quart of fresh Jersey cream,
So I thought I could see my way to realising a dream.

Nipped into the larder unseen in a lucky minute,
And nobbed some Christmas custard with eggs and brandy in it.

Knocked off the best glacé fruits from the bottom layer,
And borrowed the bottle of Noyau with a silent prayer.

Chopped up the fruits in the shed, got the milk-can,
And sloshed them up with the cream and custard according to plan.

Clapped the lid back on the can, and proceeded to tuck it
Into ice (from the duckpond) and salt in a battered bucket.

Twirled it about, and scraped it down, and made it come right,
Then nipped on parade for Christmas dinner all merry and bright.

After the pudding, pretended to fetch the cheese,
But slipped out by the back-door into – ugh! – the wintry breeze.

Dished up the stuff on a Sèvres comport (bit chipped, you know,
The one mother got for eighteen pence in Ragbag Row).

Further adorned it with lashings of flaunting finery,
Namely, some gorgeous leaves and grapes from our quite big vinery.

Carried it in, to the general stupefaction,
But the overfed blighters soon got back into action.

Just how it got there was dimly felt to be puzzling.
But they lost no time in getting on with the guzzling.

Then with one accord they lifted their liqueur brandy,
And shouting with laughter, proceeded to pelt me with anything
    handy.

THERE WAS A WOMAN ONCE...

(A Fragment)

There was a woman once who had these things:
Wild valley-lilies and nightingales,
Vines and willows, peachtrees and apricots,
Still beauty, wonderful beauty, abundance.

An ancient house and garden, families
Of dear neighbours with well-loved books and instruments,
Voices known as her own, children and grandmothers
Shared, days of delight and wisdom, the priest moving
Loved and loving among them; immemorial
A vast church with all their dead, hallowed and sleeping...

THERE WAS A WOMAN ONCE

(A Fragment)

There was a woman once: not long ago.
It is all different now, my dear: but you also
Sent out your soul to gardens you never knew,
Children you did not bear, and beloved
Neighbours and lovers whom somehow you never met.
We all do it: idyll or misery now notwithstanding.

LEWIS APPEARS

*(Apropos of C.S. Lewis's move to Cambridge, and his
possible effect on Leavis and the Logical Positivists)*

Lewis appears, the Trojan Dinosaur,
Eggs of ambivalence distend his Maur.
What meant the Fathers to convey him in?
I wish I knew the Mind of those grave Min.

*"Maur" is "maw", misspelt to avoid a false rhyme with "dinosaur";
"Min" is the plural of "man" in Essex dialect. – R.P.*

THE BEARDED BABE

I dreamed I found a white-haired boy,
A strong babe of a year.
He smiled with health, he did not cry,
And milk-white was his hair.
And lovely his bright limbs appeared,
And fair were all his ways:
But on his chin a wool-white beard
Like those of ancient days.

STRANGE ROOM, STRANGE GARDEN

The room is so big and sad wherever I find it,
That sorrowful room that is not there,
Opening from a familiar house: half-blind it
Rises to a clerestory dim and bare,
With shallow lunette windows like a riding-school,
Mouldy and peeling walls and stagnant air:
This is some rotten lacuna in the mind of a fool.

But the extra-garden is better than real: it grows
Somewhere within the everyday rood that is mine:
I find it now and then in a dream, and it knows
I have come to my own and begins to wave and shine,
With bigger than life-size fruit, and flowers more real
Than any I grow, so truly they flourish, so fine:
But only the blessed could tell you the bliss that I feel.

HIGH SUMMER

Last winter was so long and cruel
We thought it never would be done;
The never-ending bills for fuel,
The long-drawn pining for the sun:

And on and on the scolding wind
Scoured all our springtime hopes away:
And when that dropped, the sour unkind
Late frost came in and had its way.

Then May, as ever, cold and dry,
And dripping June was dry and cold.
We looked no longer in the sky,
But drooped, and knew that we were old.

Dry sticks, our vaunted passion-flower:
Brown brush, the myrtle: winter-sweet
That in dead winter makes a bower
Shed all its promise round its feet.

THE HALF-REMEMBERED TUNE

Striving to recall some Air
Embodying the fine, the fair
Sure vision of the whole, we yet
Remember only it was sweet:

So in the central void of mind
Where sense is empty, thought is blind,
Both omnipresent and alone
We feel the music of the One.

CHORUS

(from a Prologue to a Nativity Play)

Yes, sit down, Mother,
You must be tired.
Father, you sit down too.
Watch for a little what we do.
We haven't found the way back yet,
We're far from home: but can't forget
The pull of God, the ache, the call.
Our hearts know Love makes up for all.